I0462652

Mandala Coloring Book: Great Variety of Mixed Mandala Designs to Color for Relaxation Stress Relieving

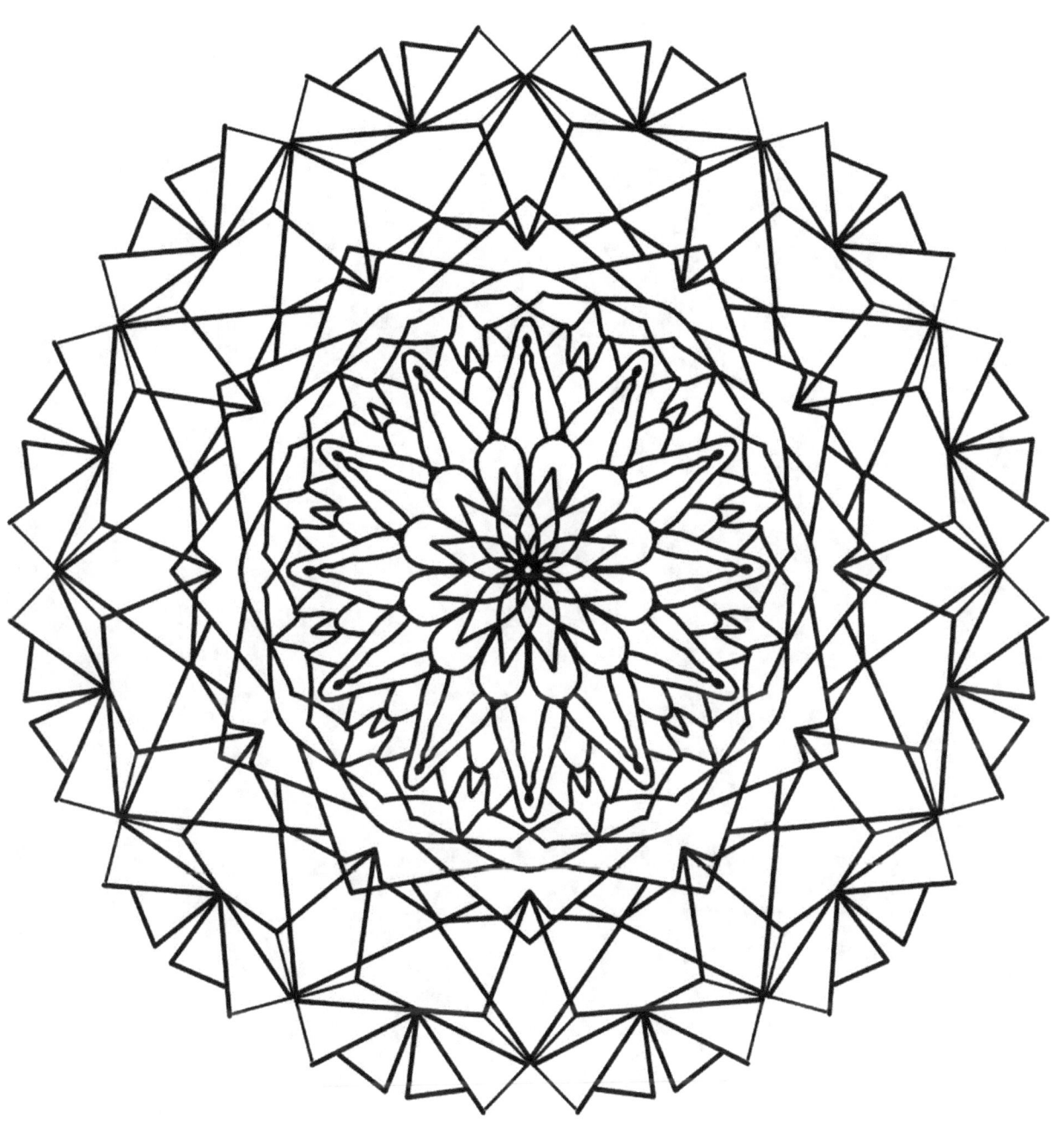

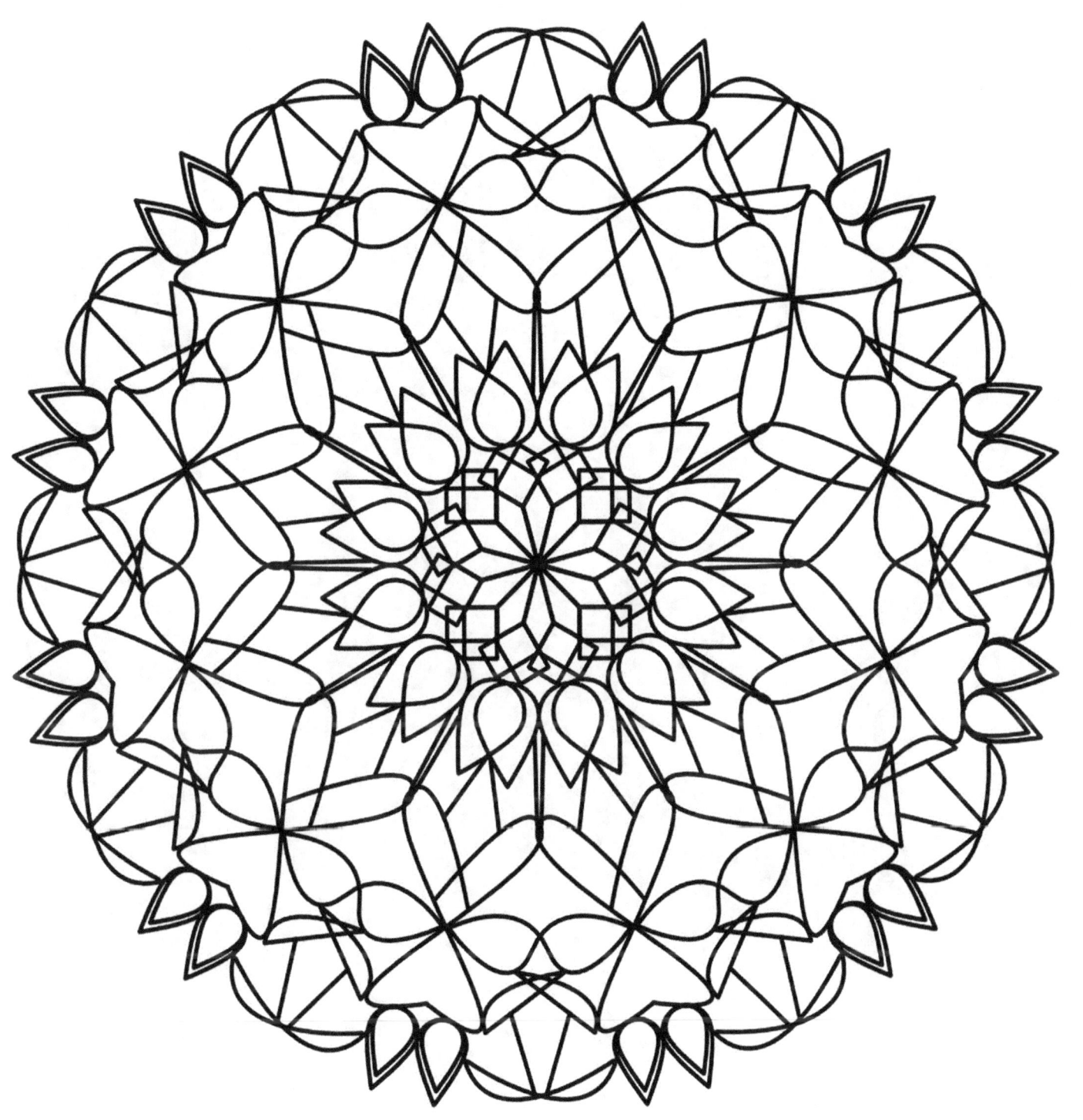

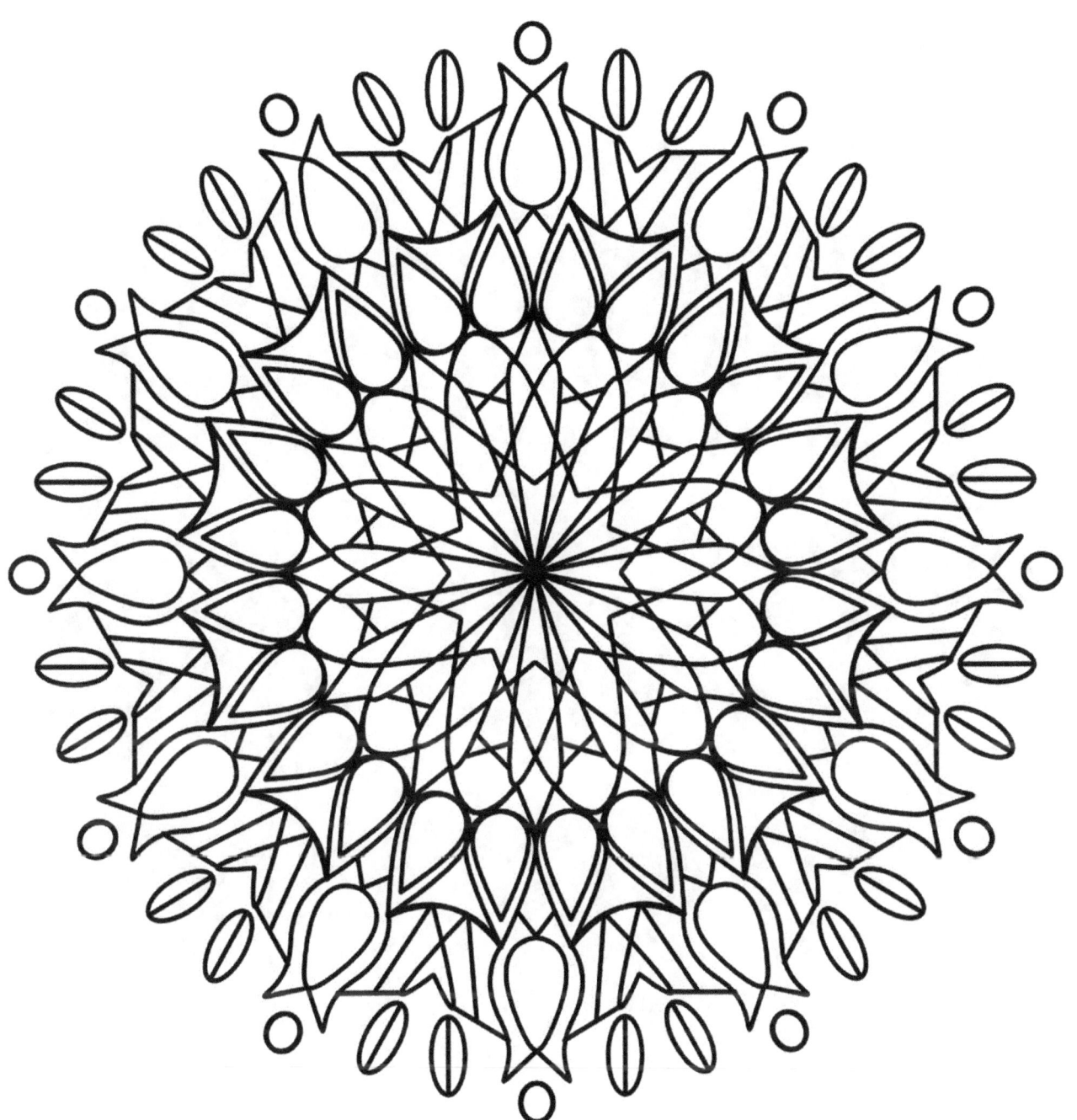

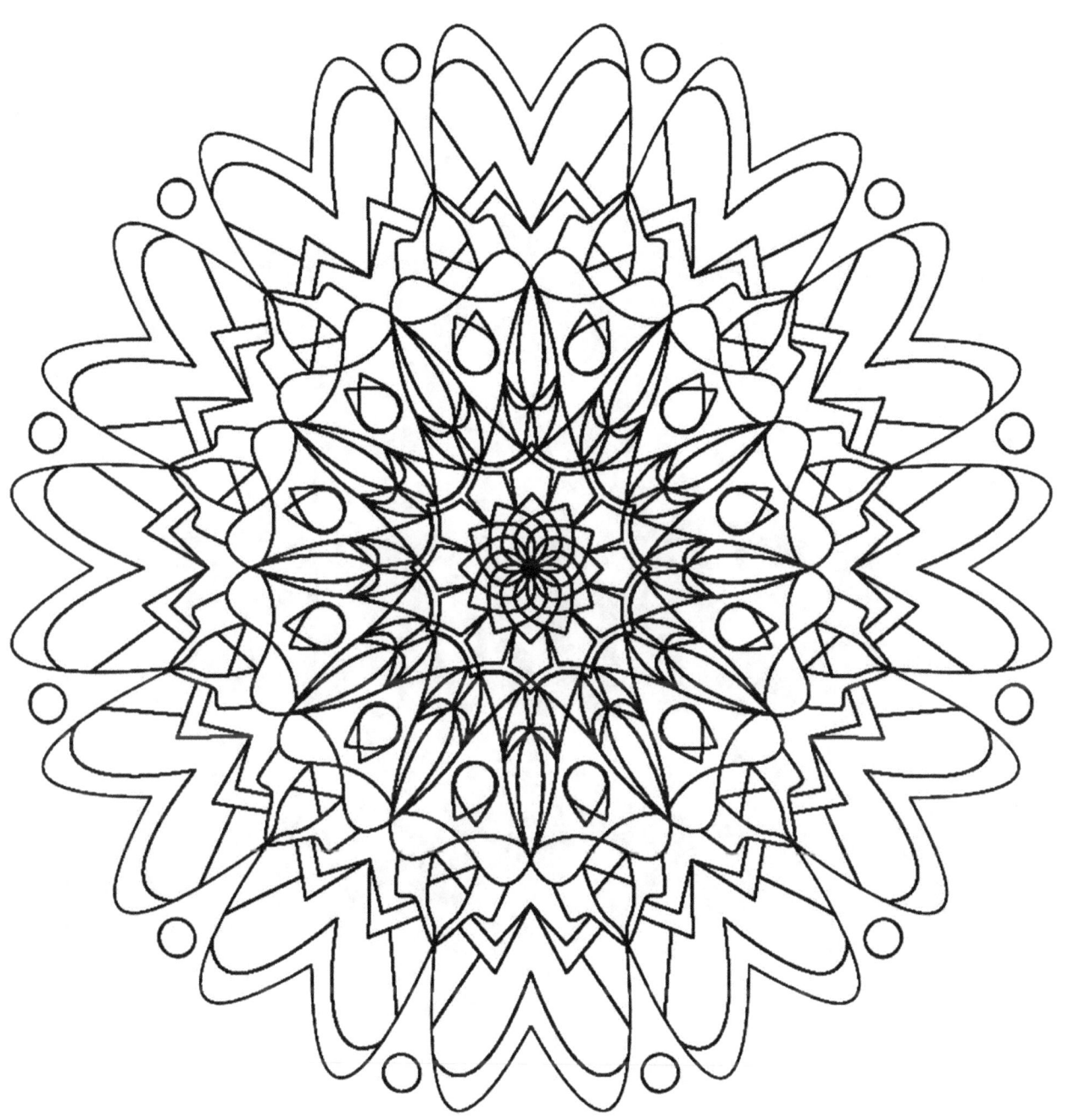

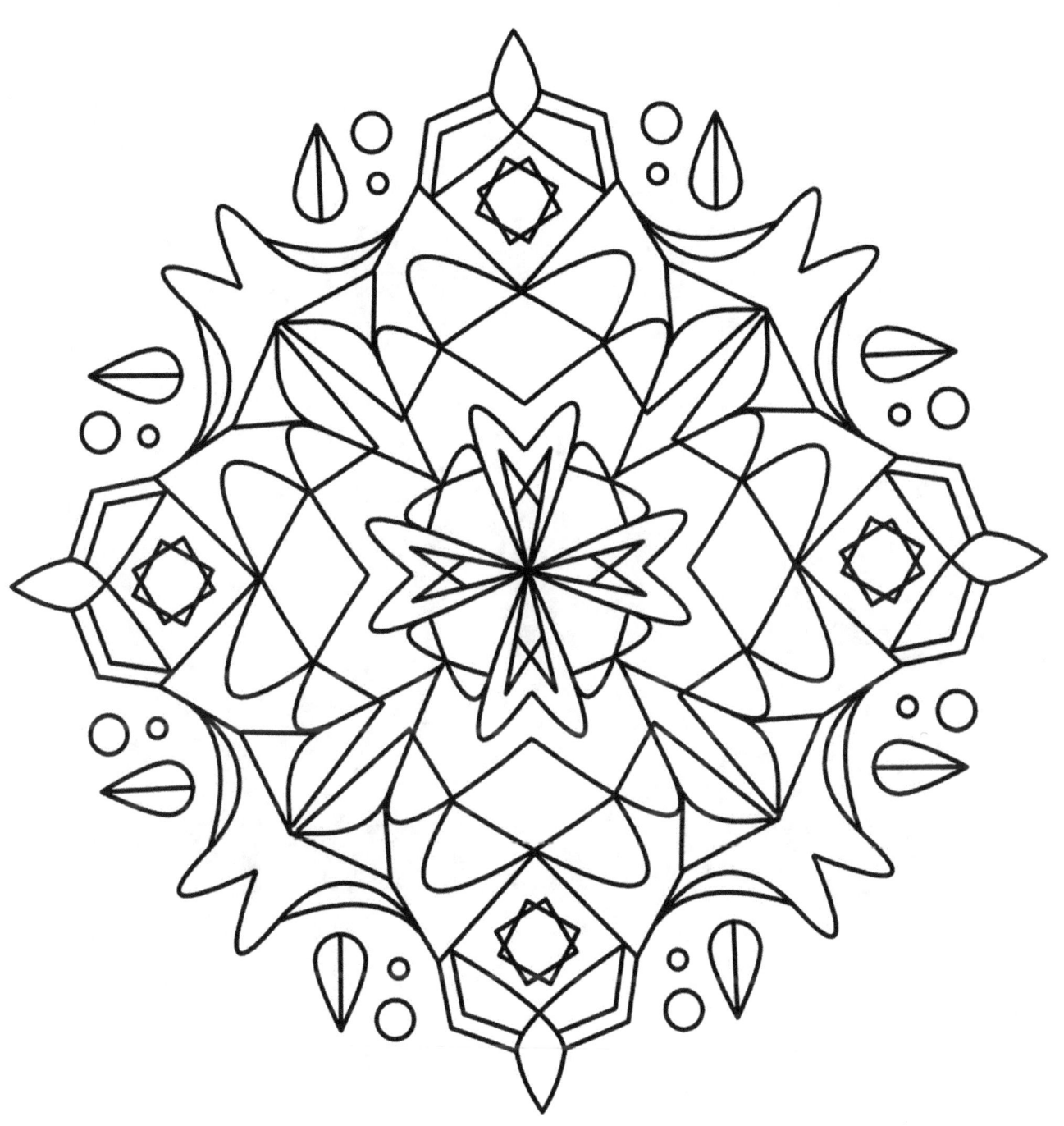

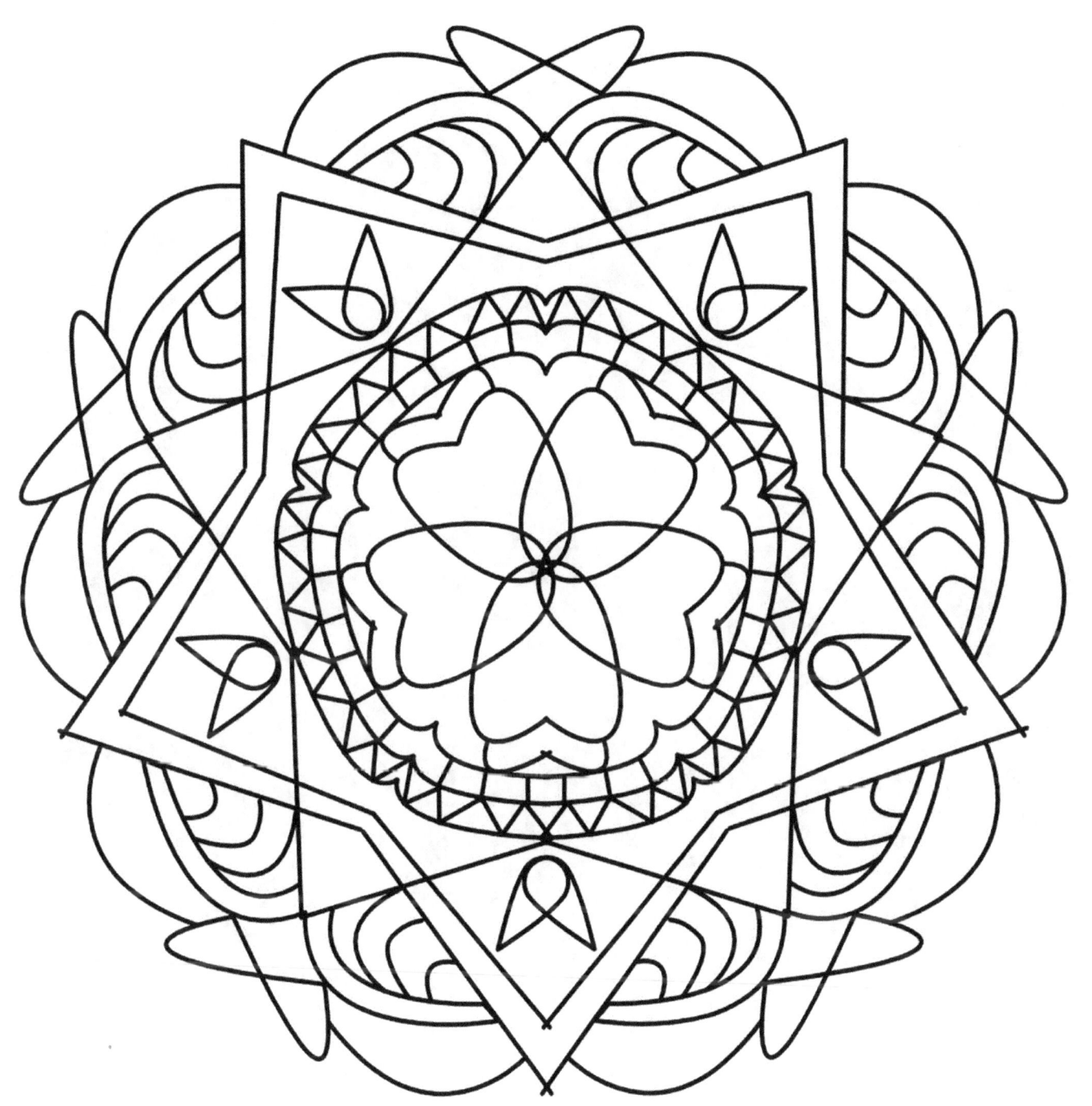

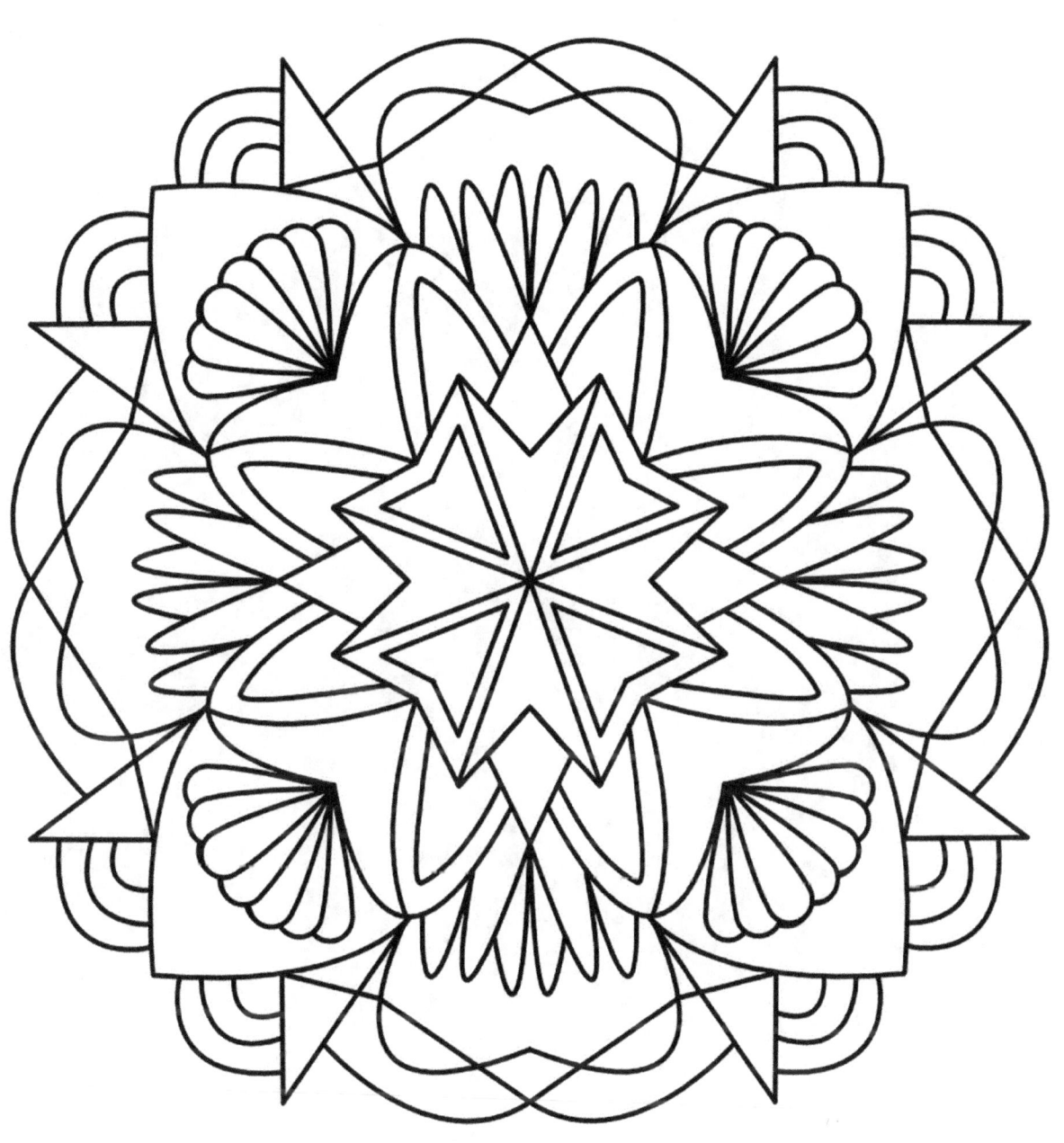

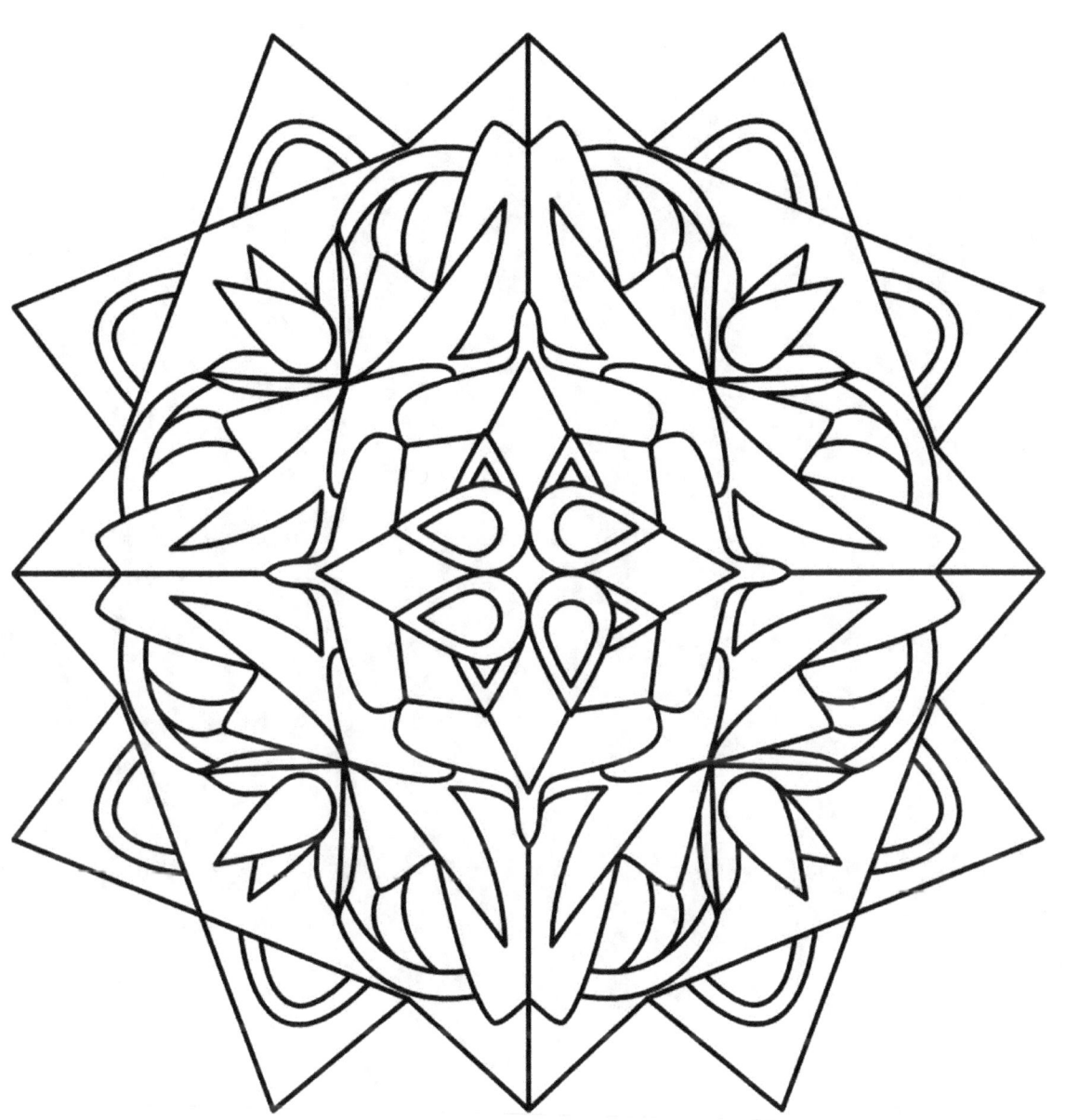

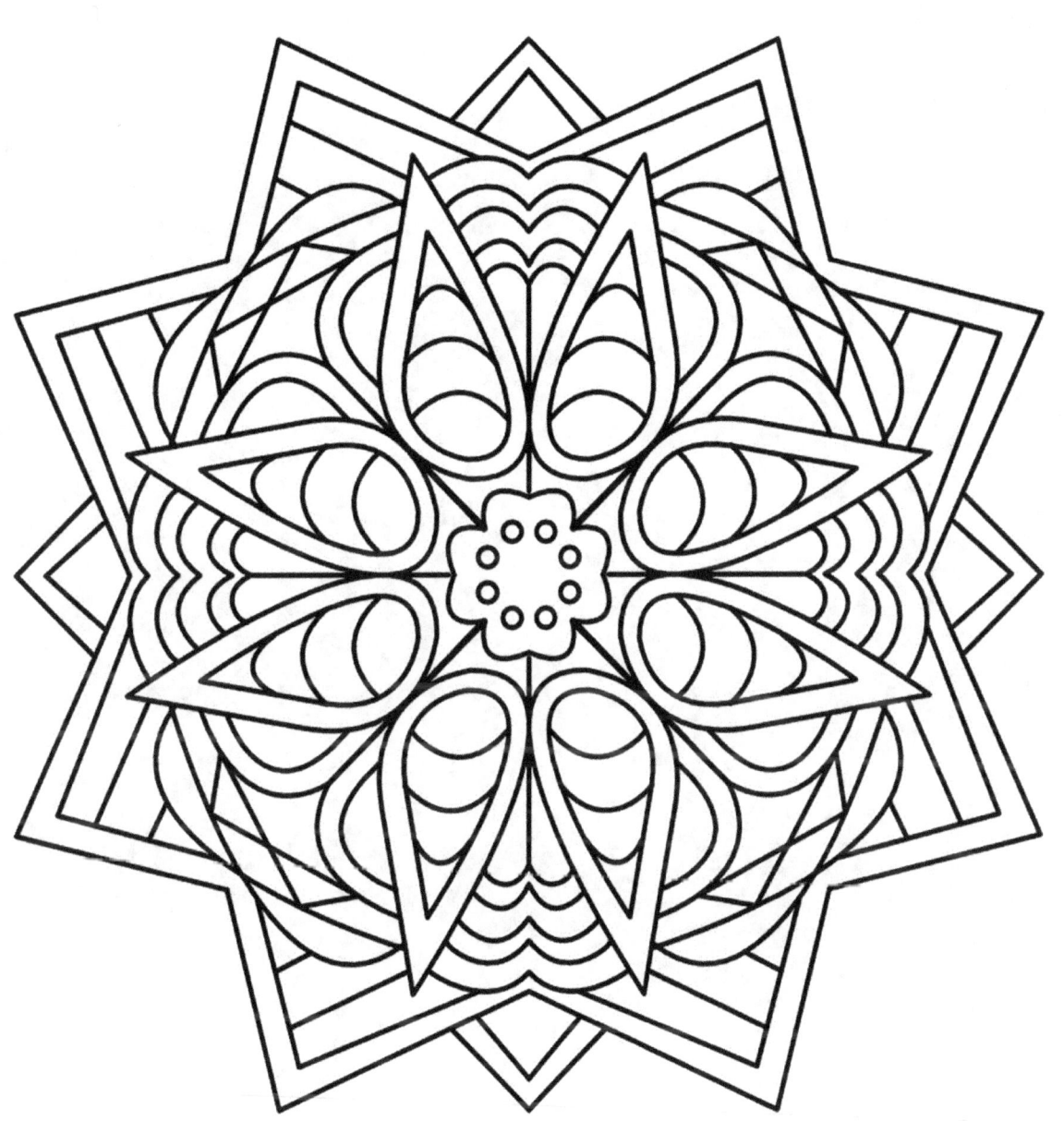

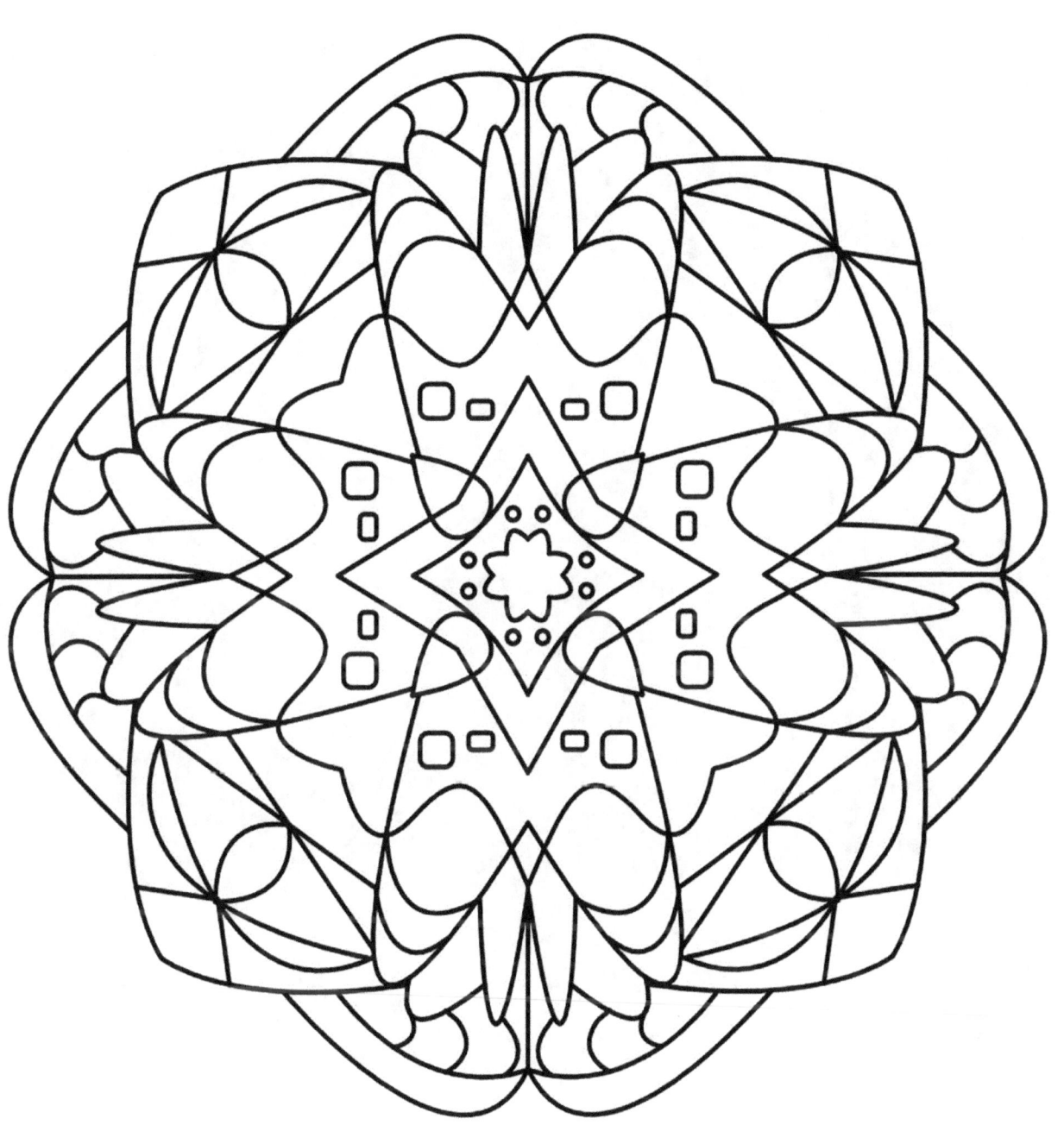

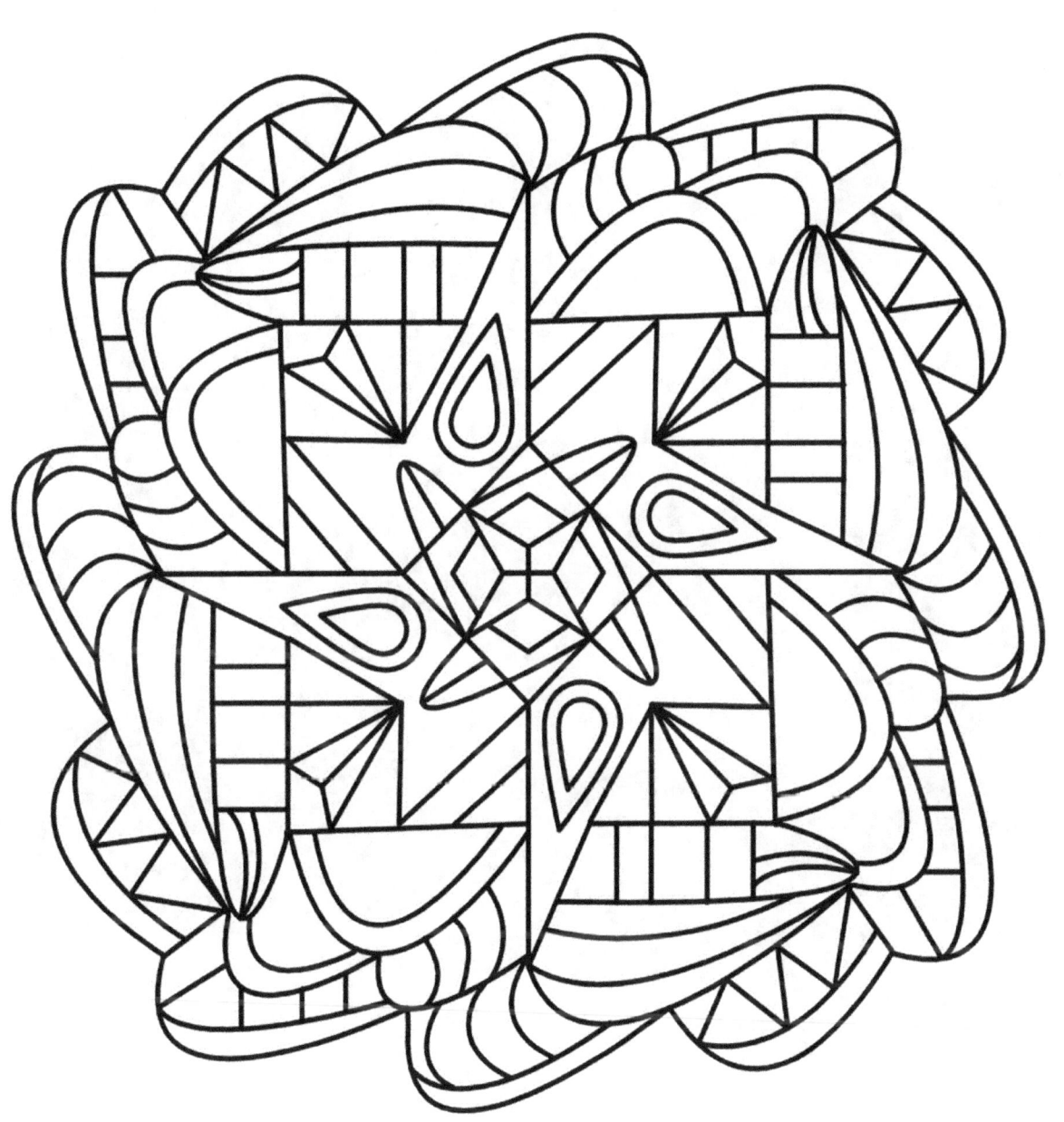

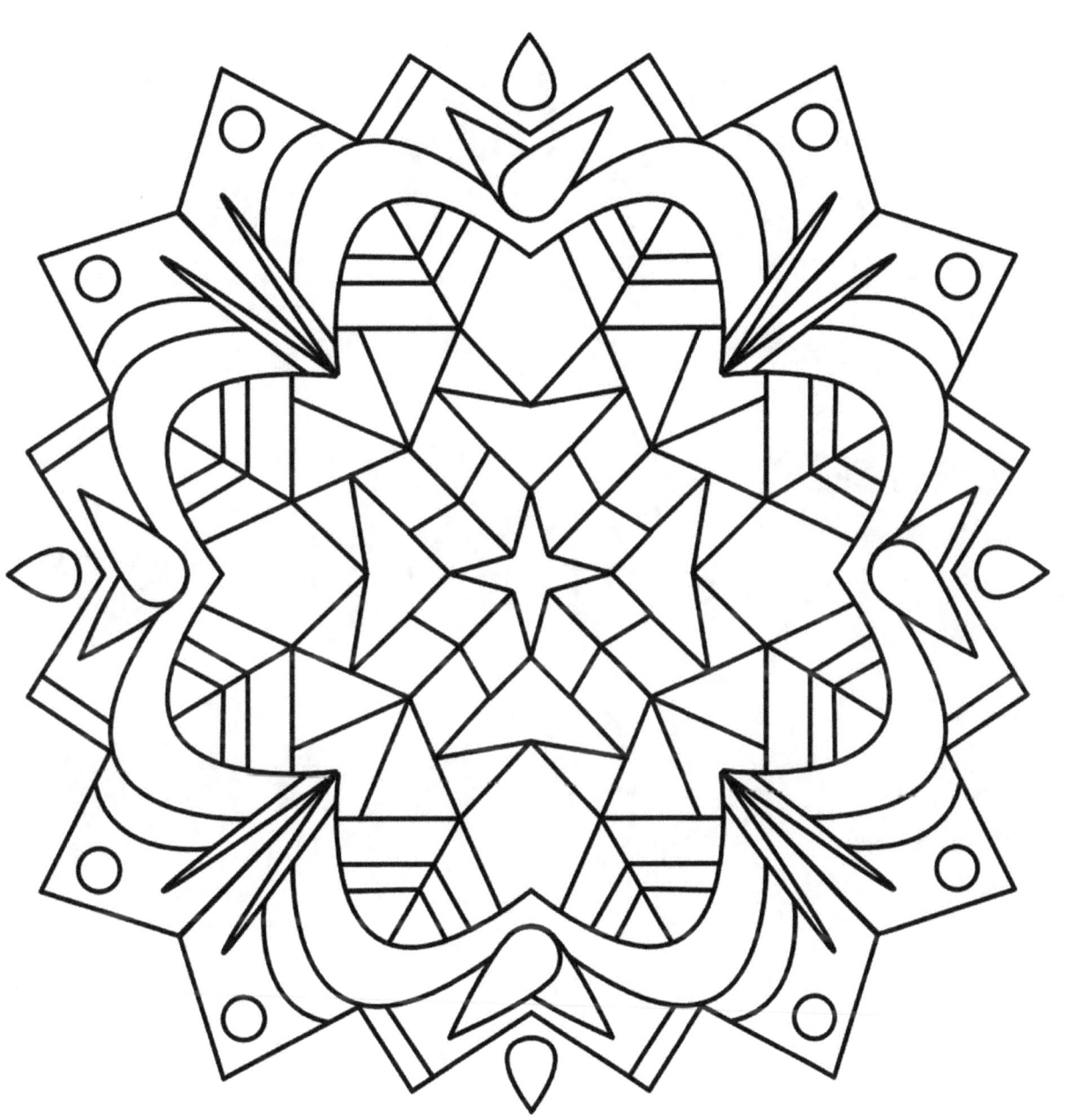

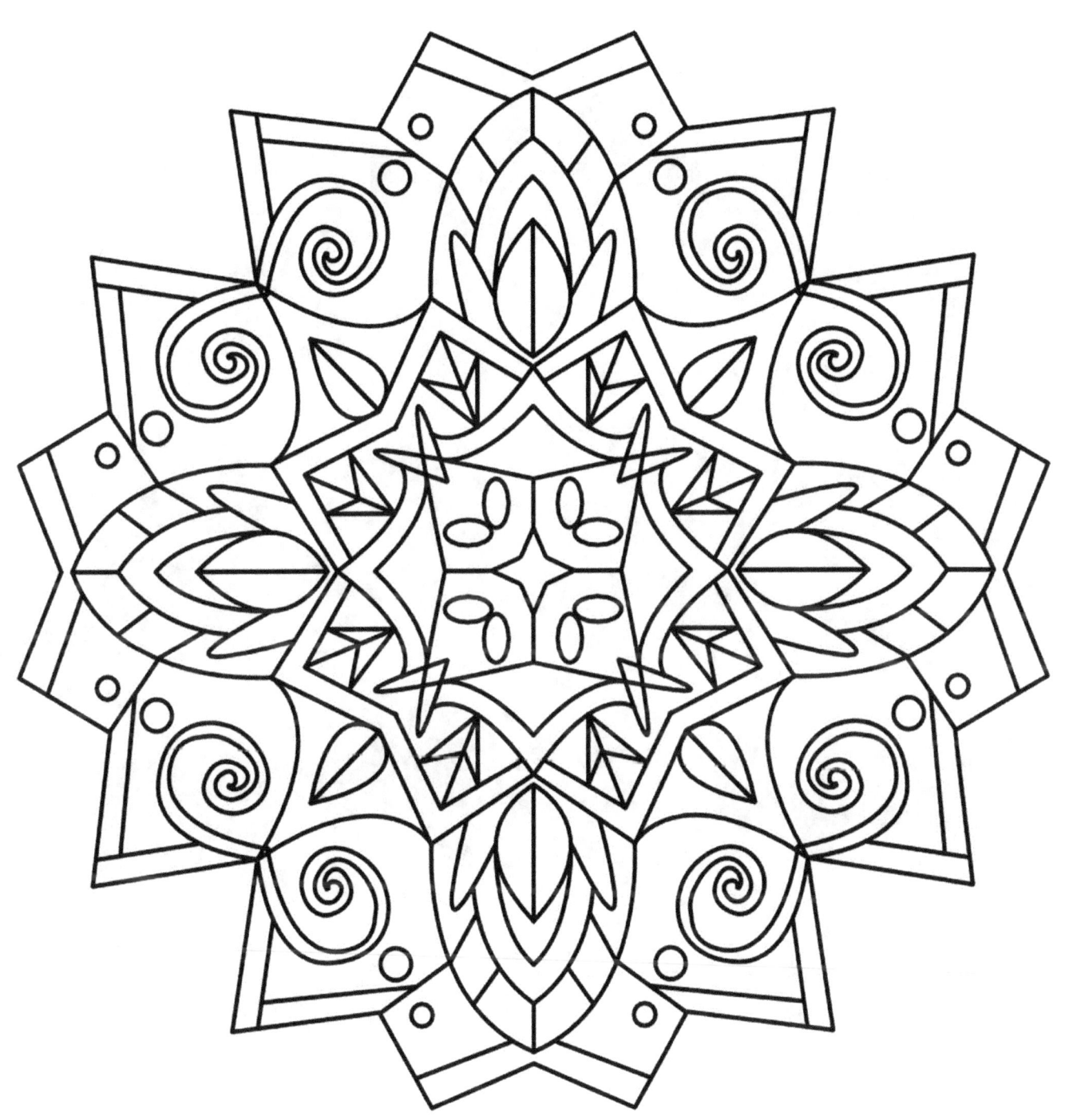

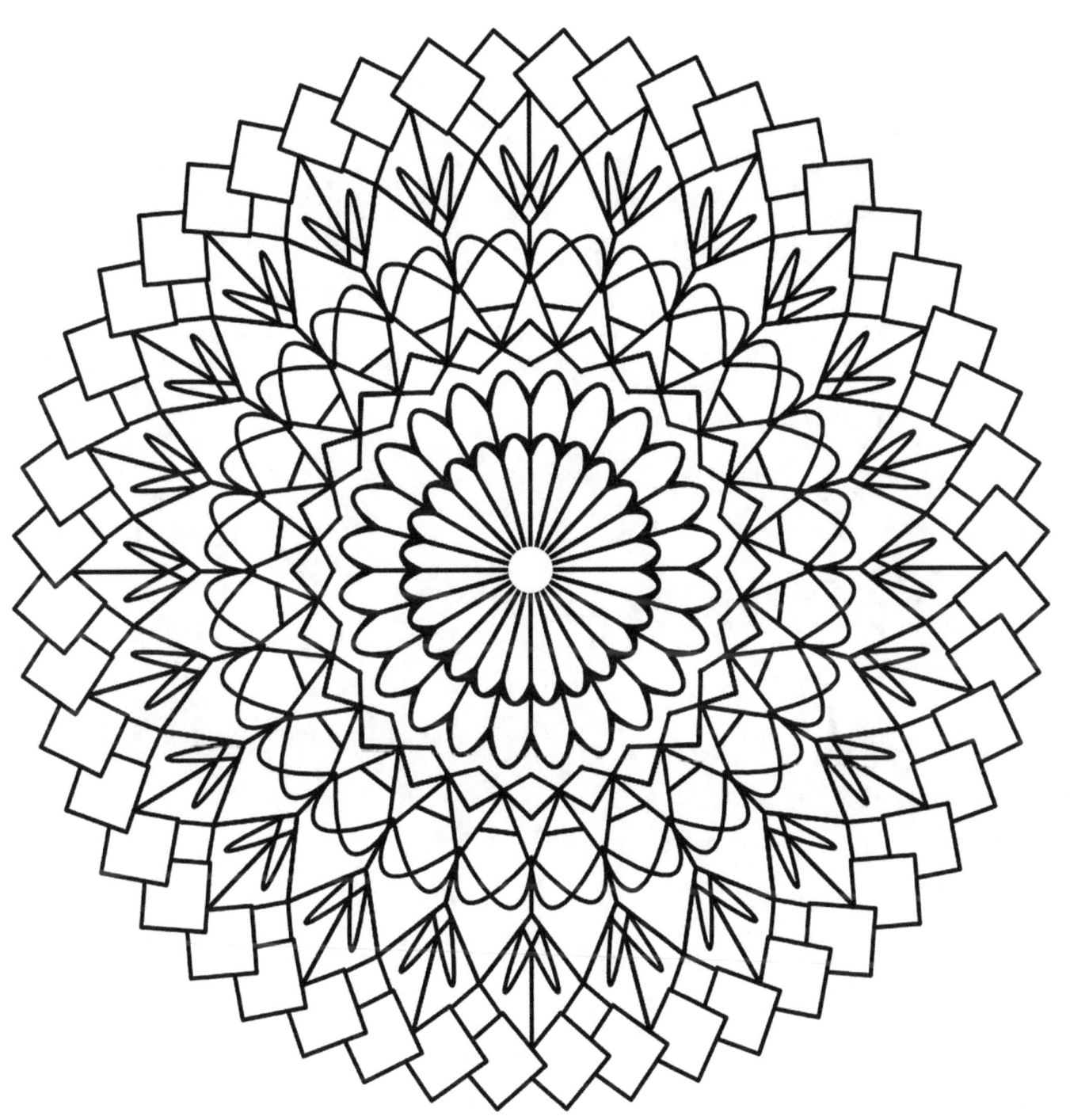

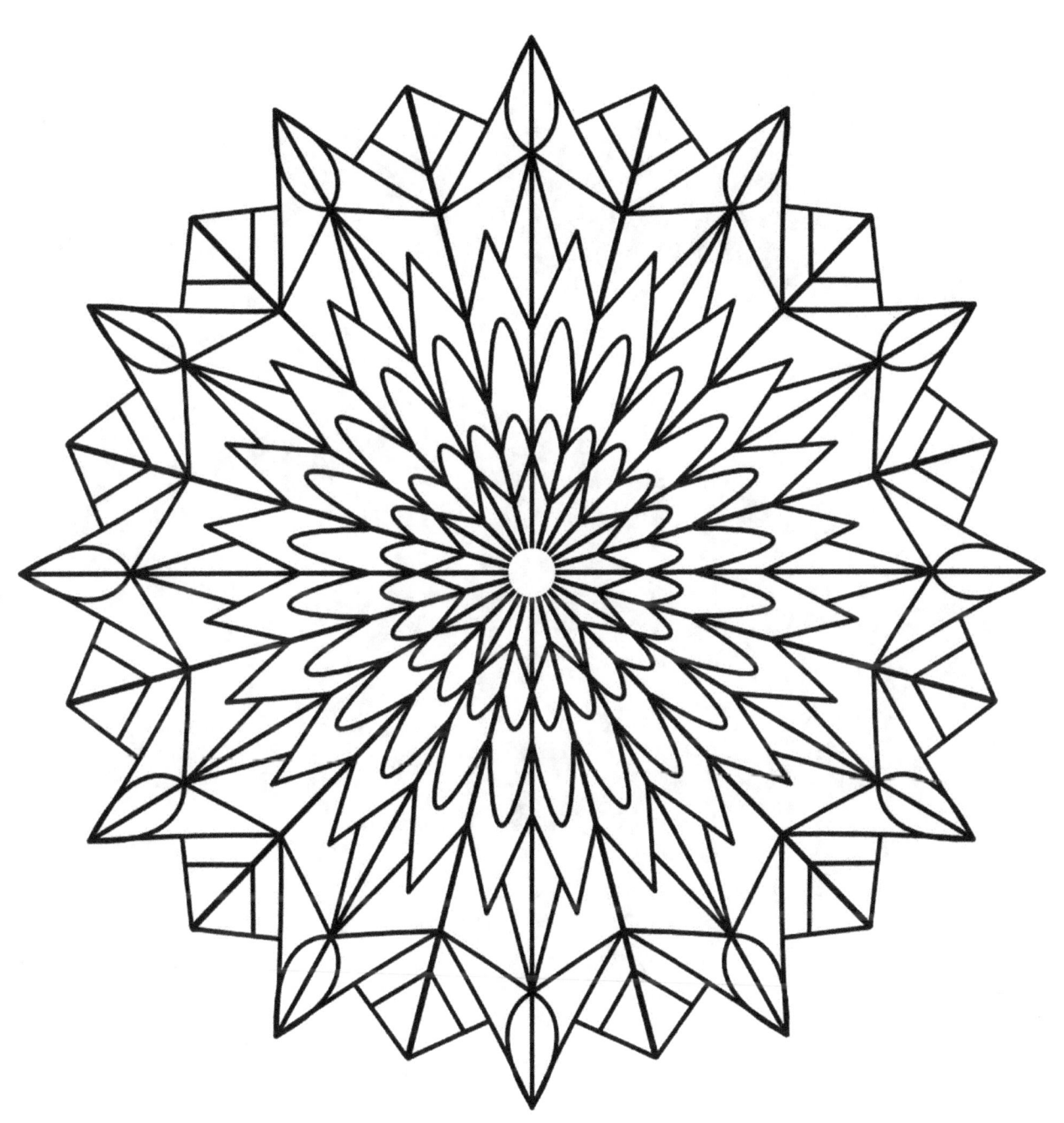

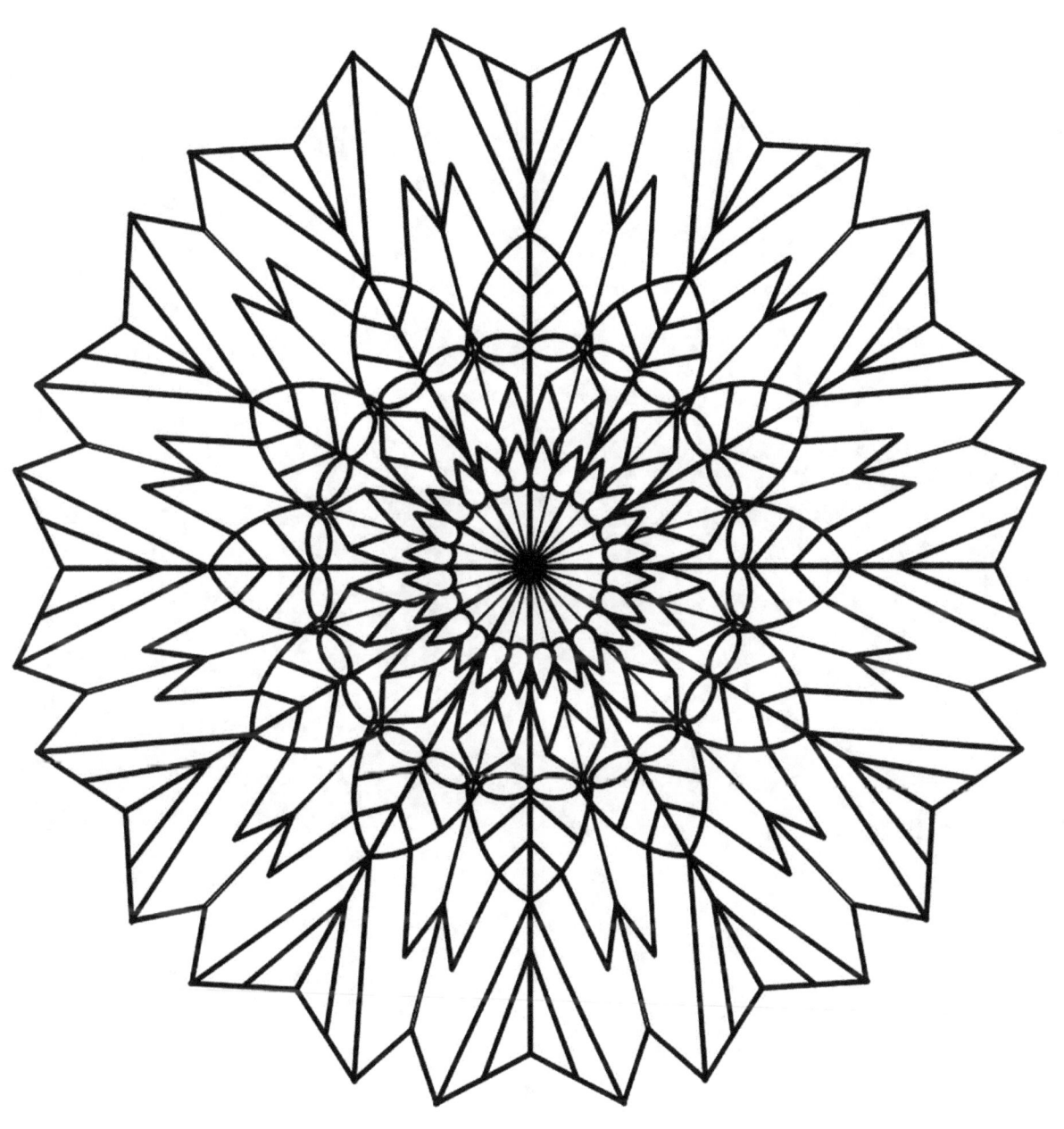

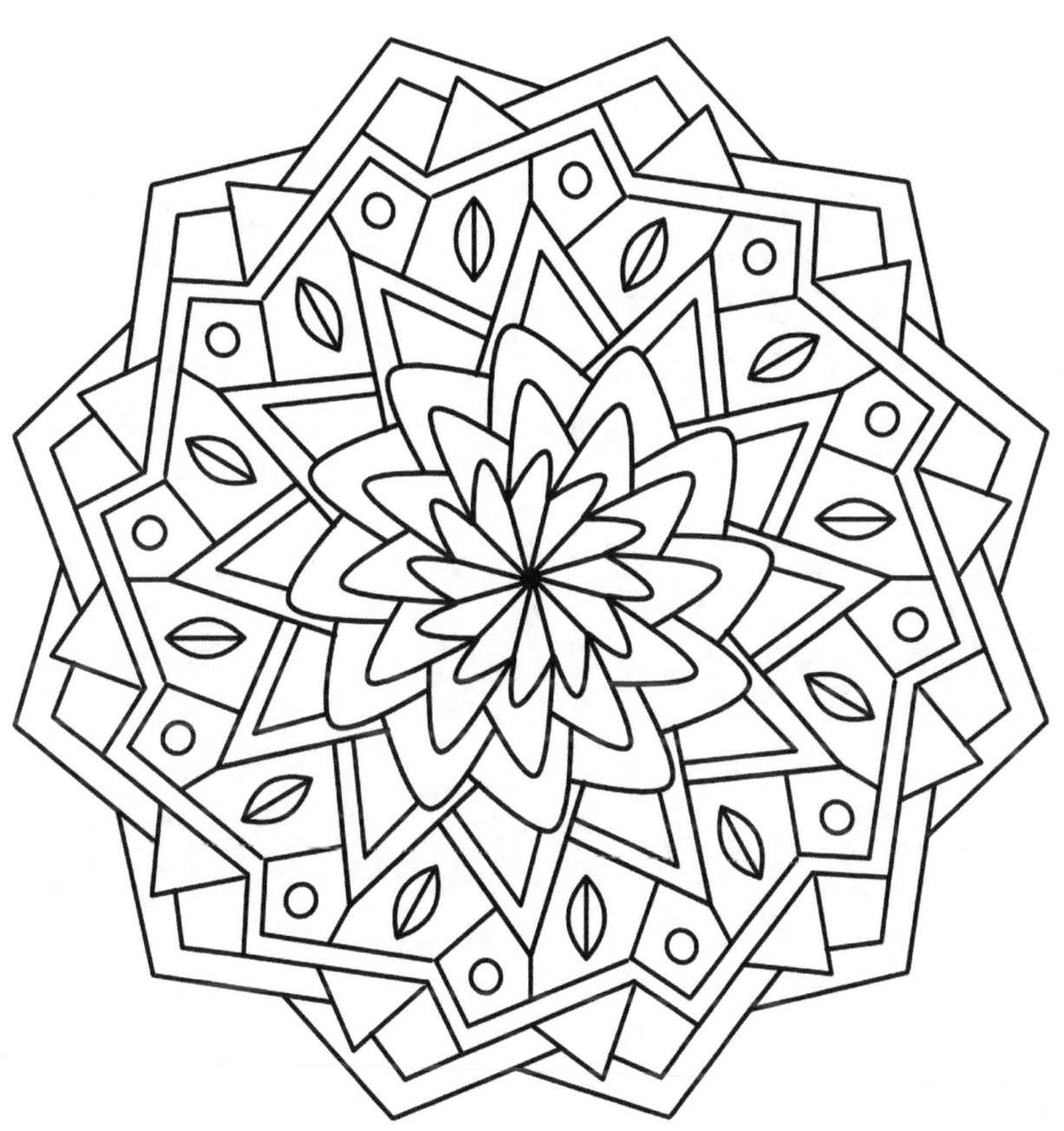

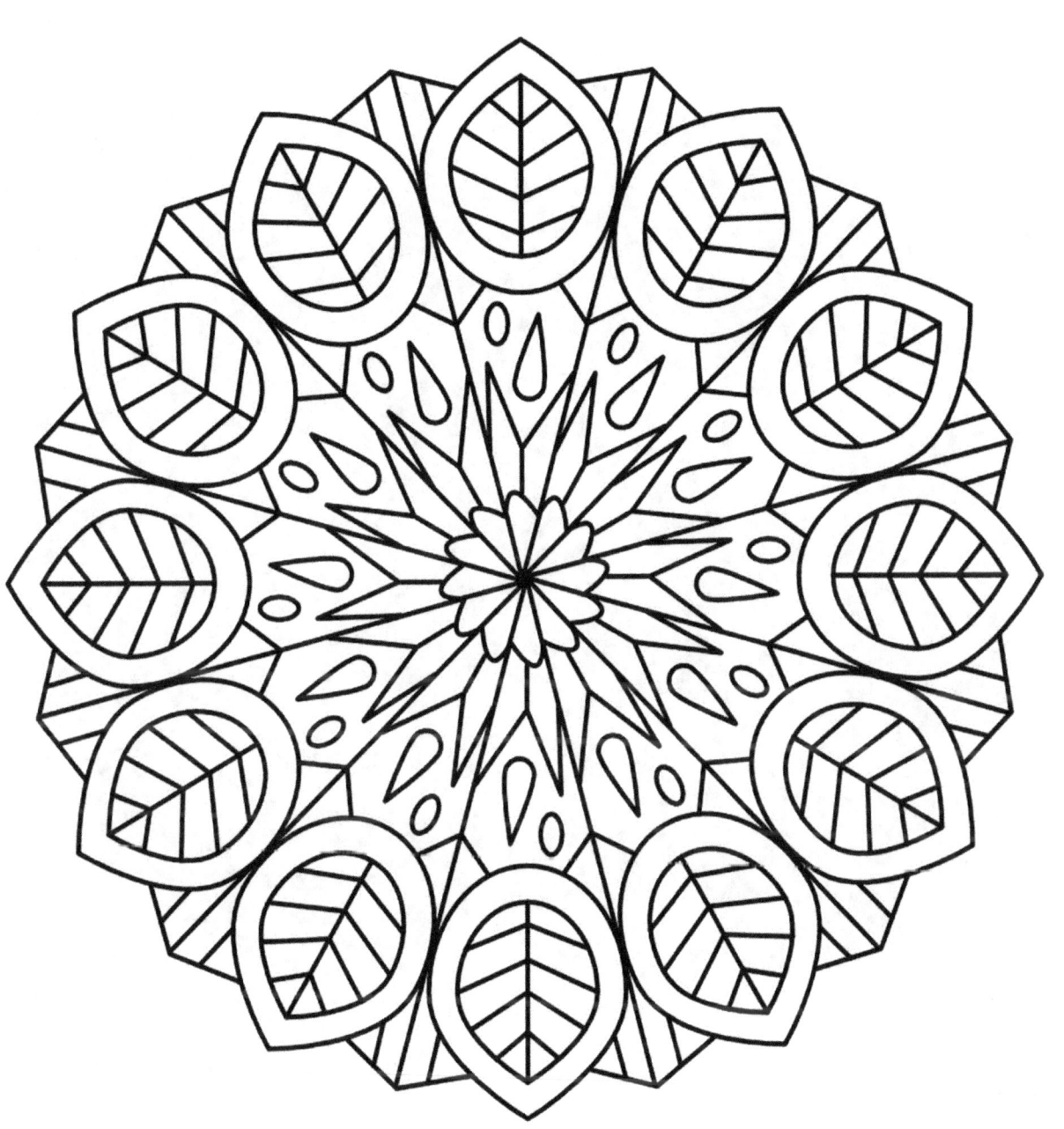

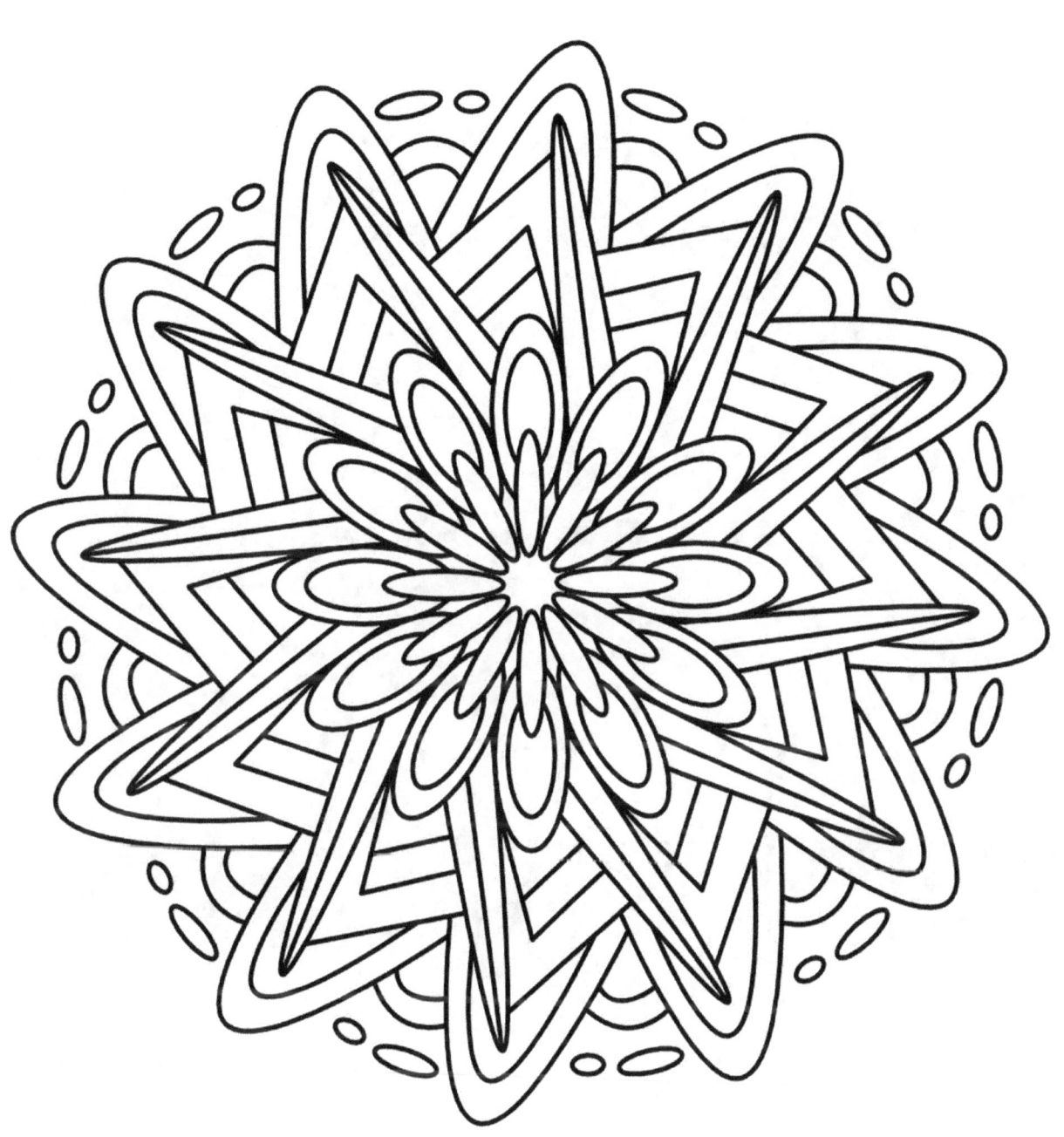

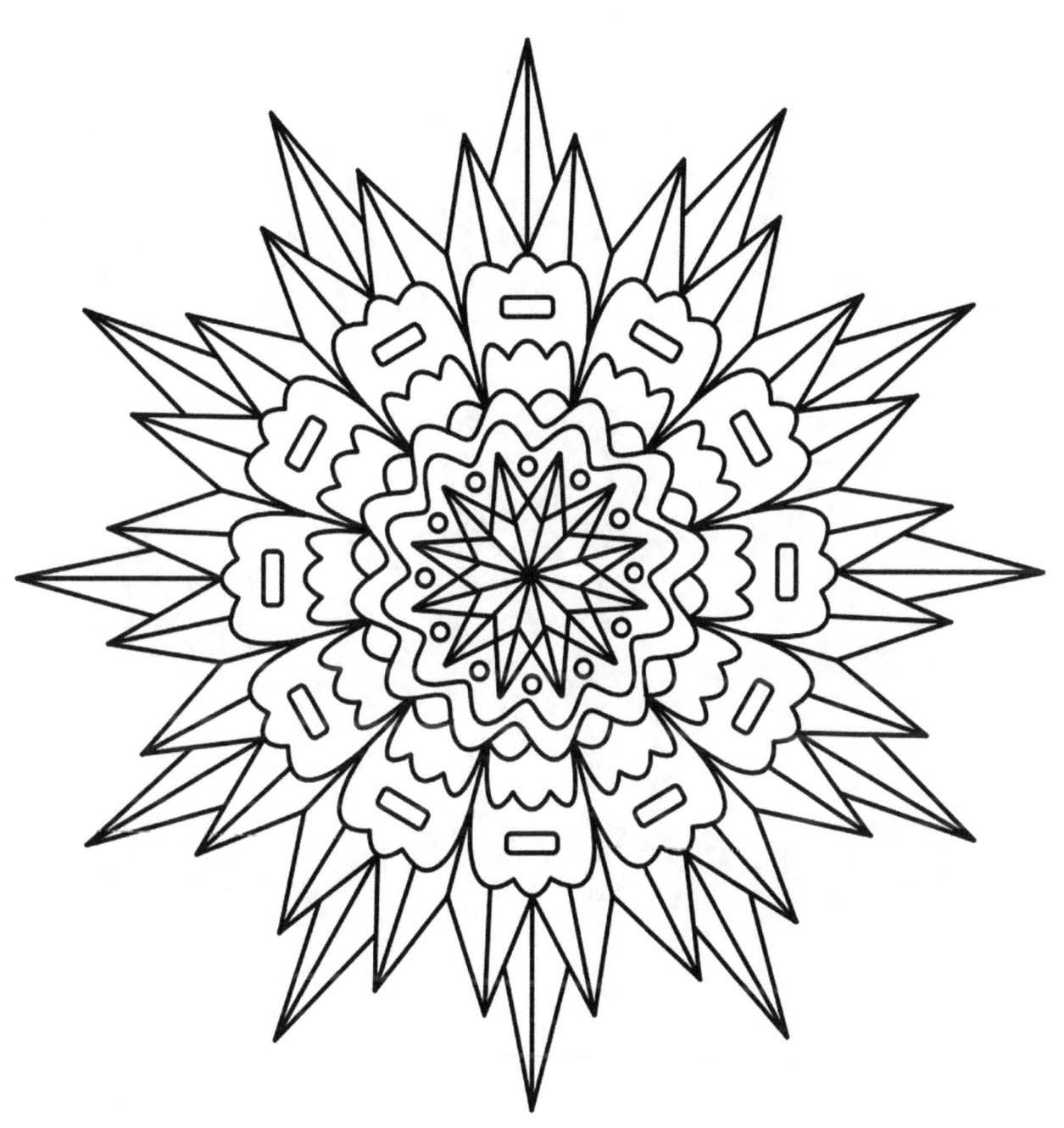

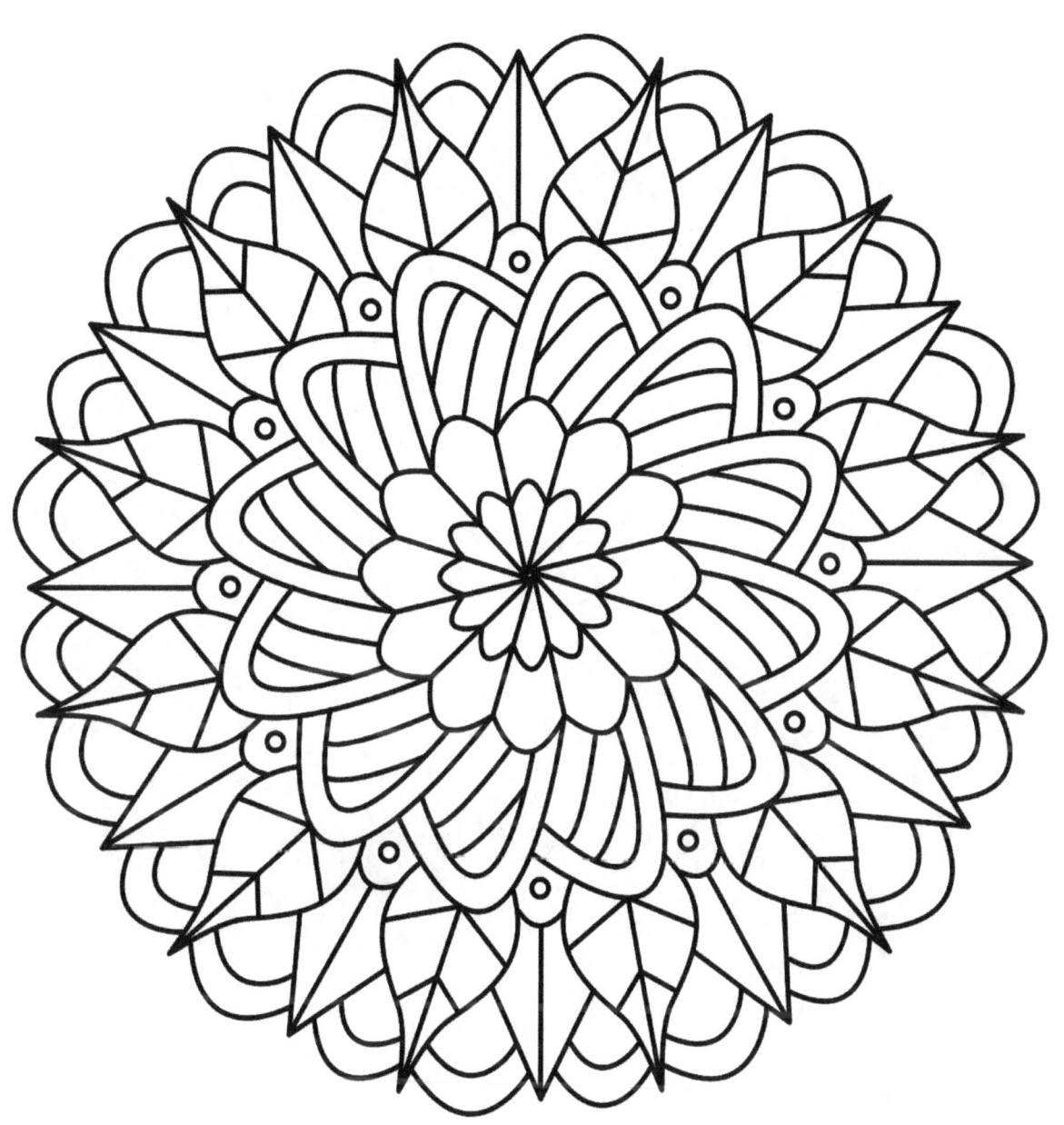

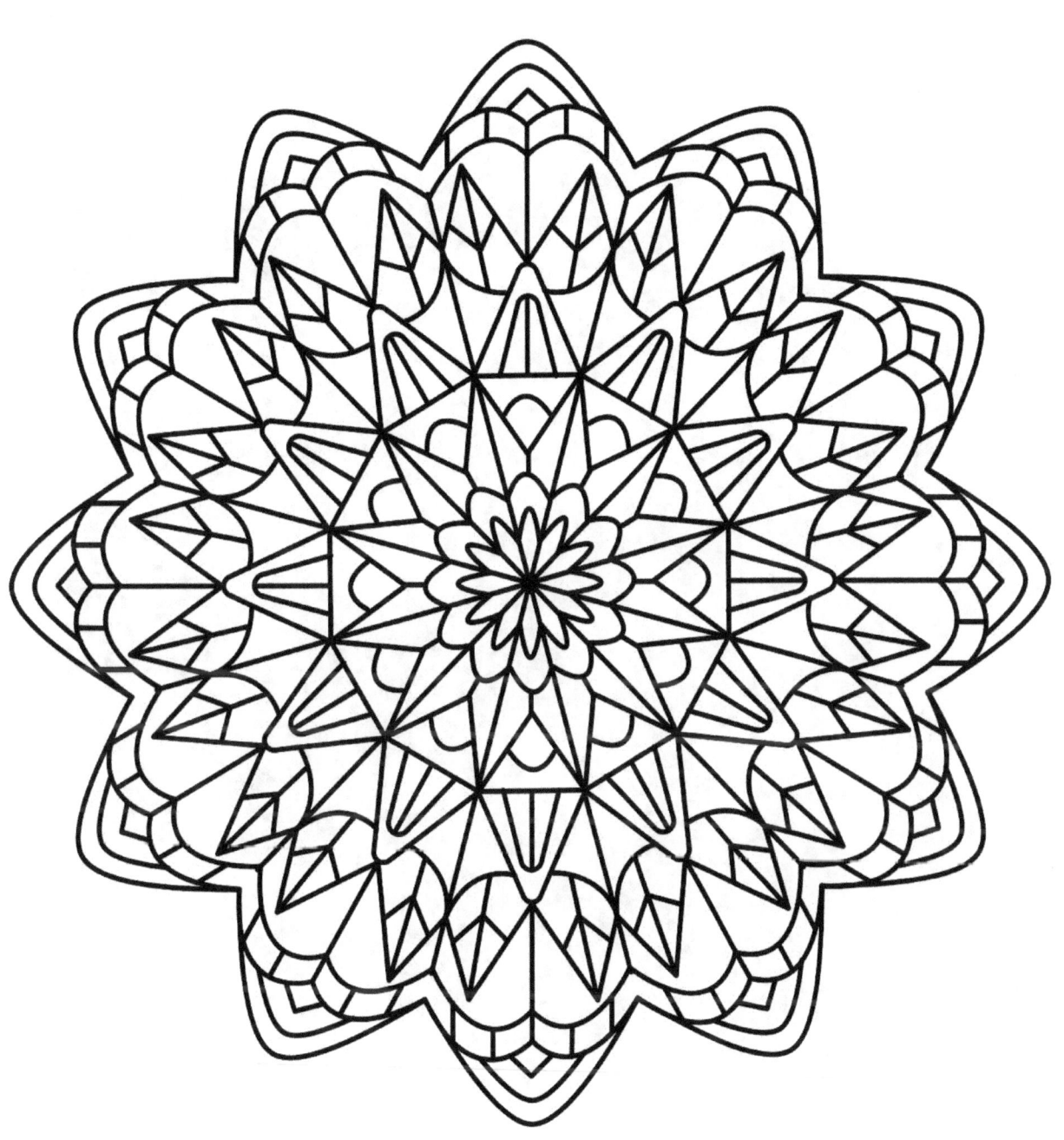

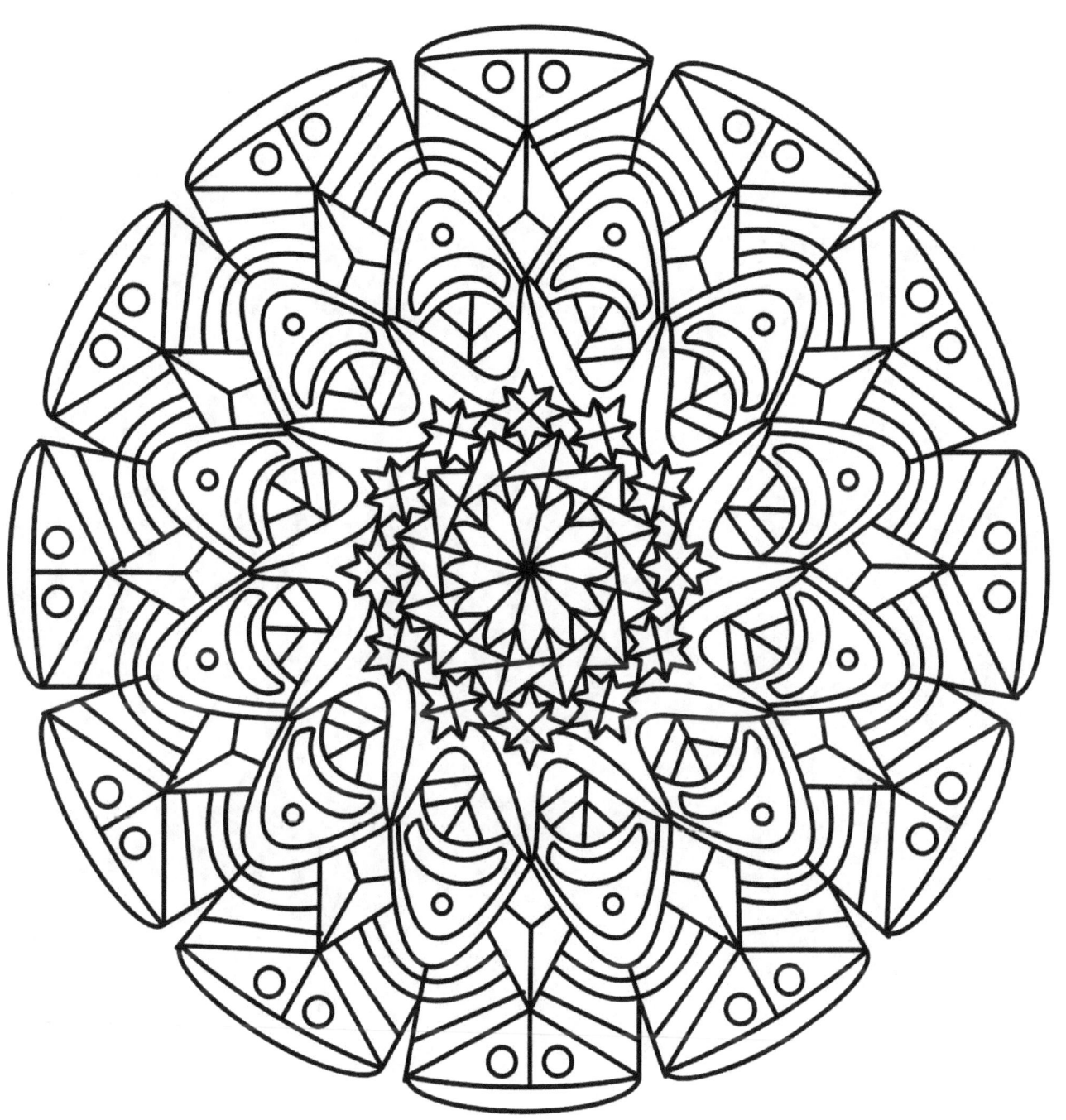

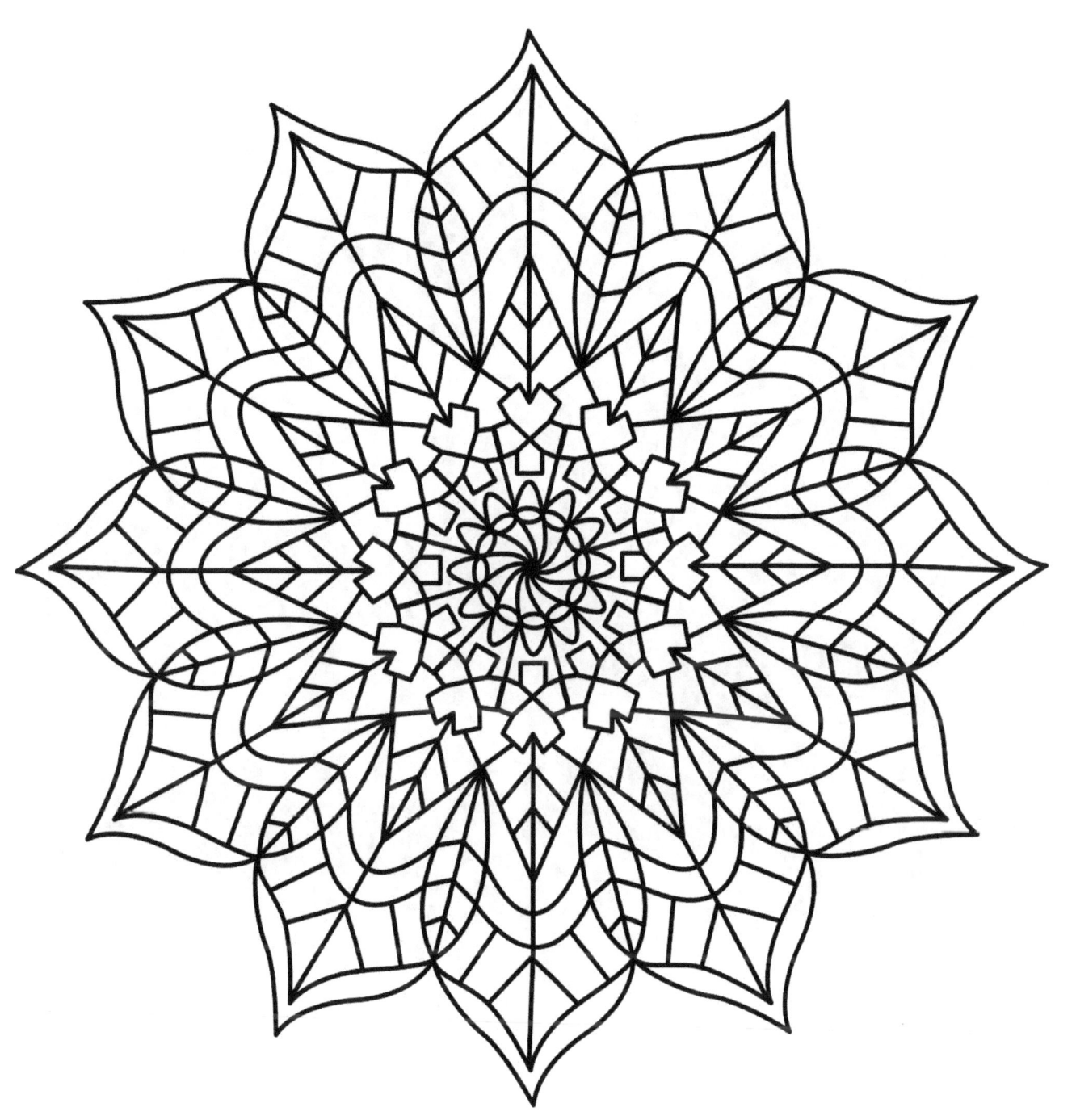

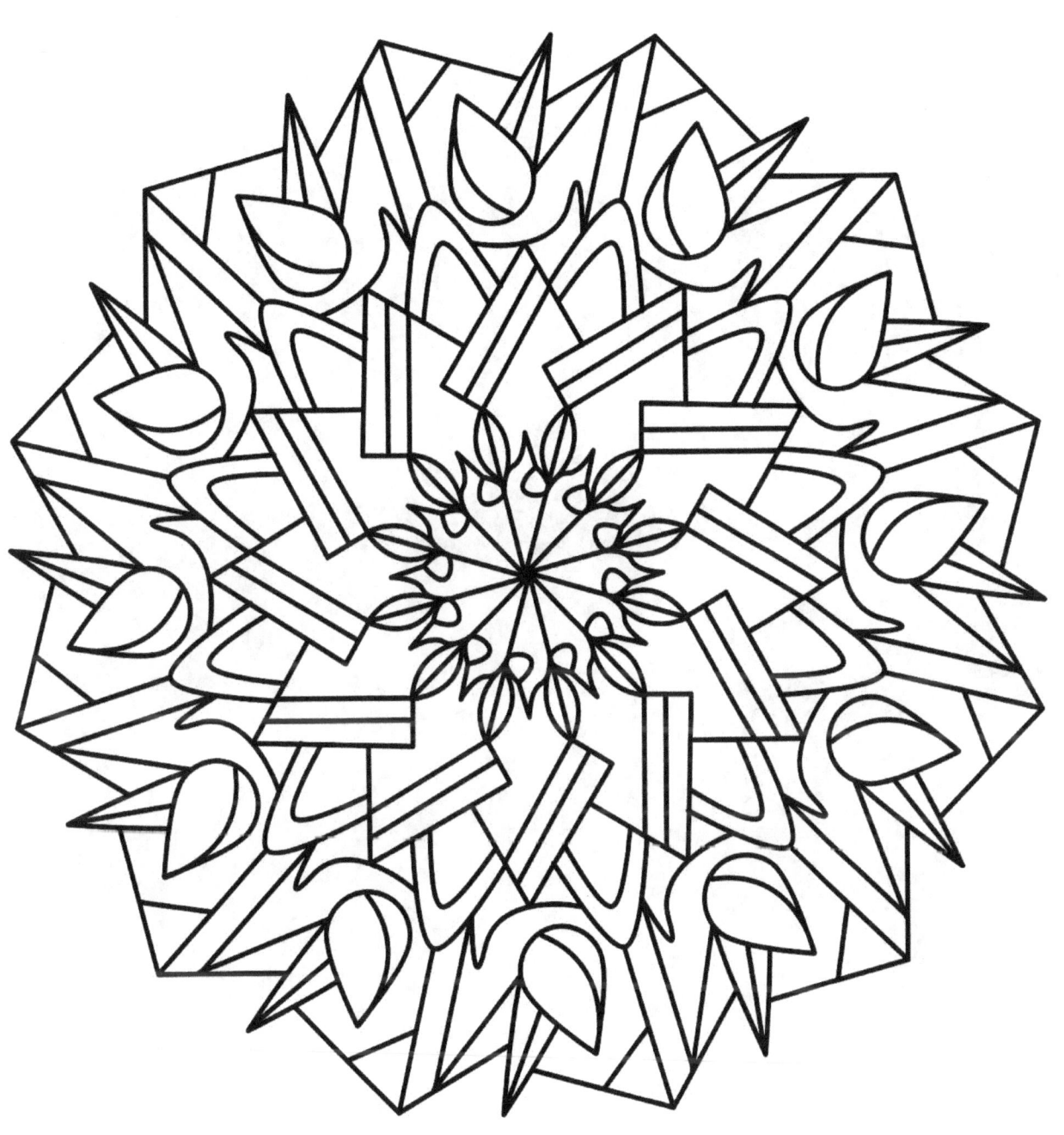

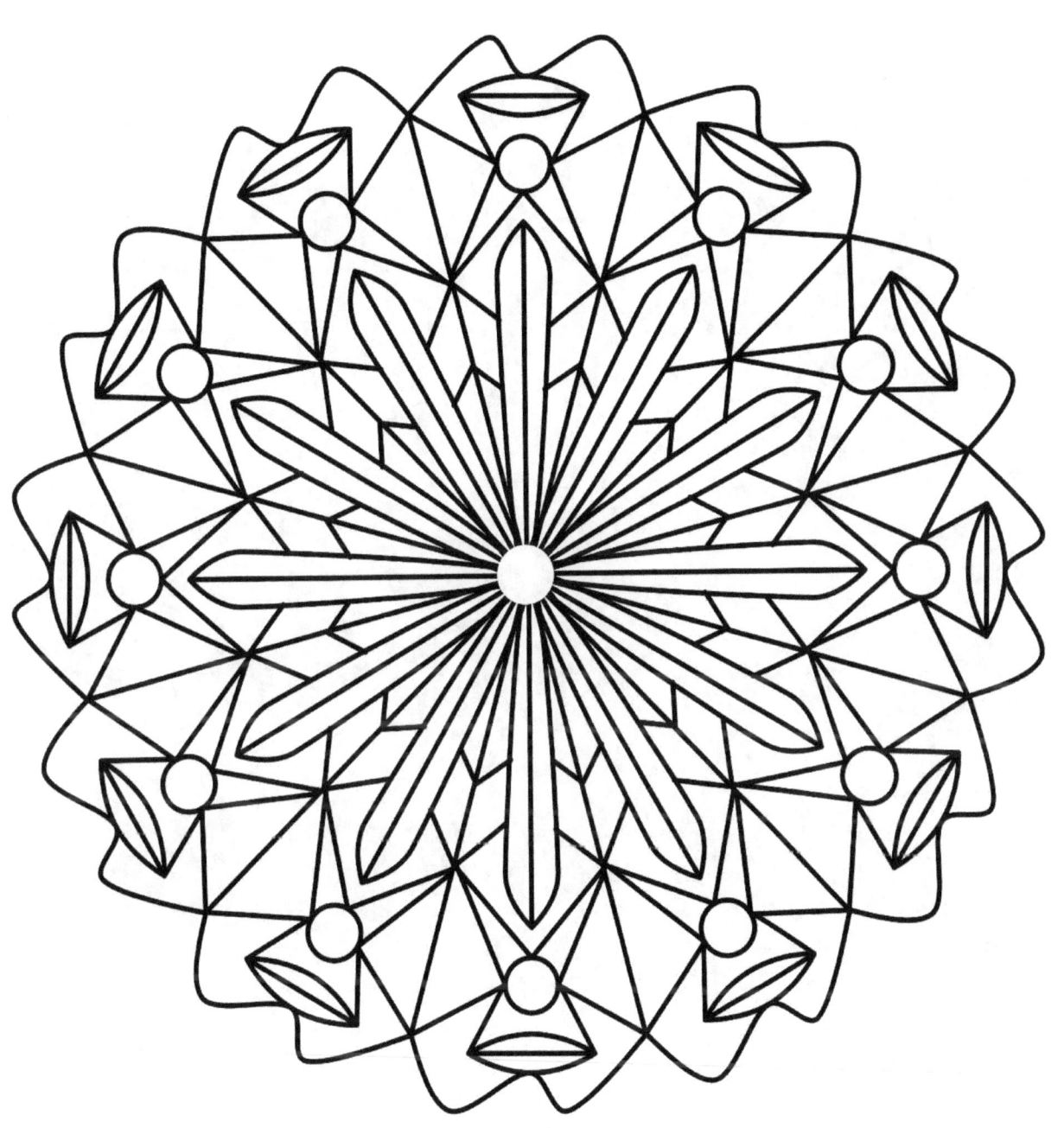

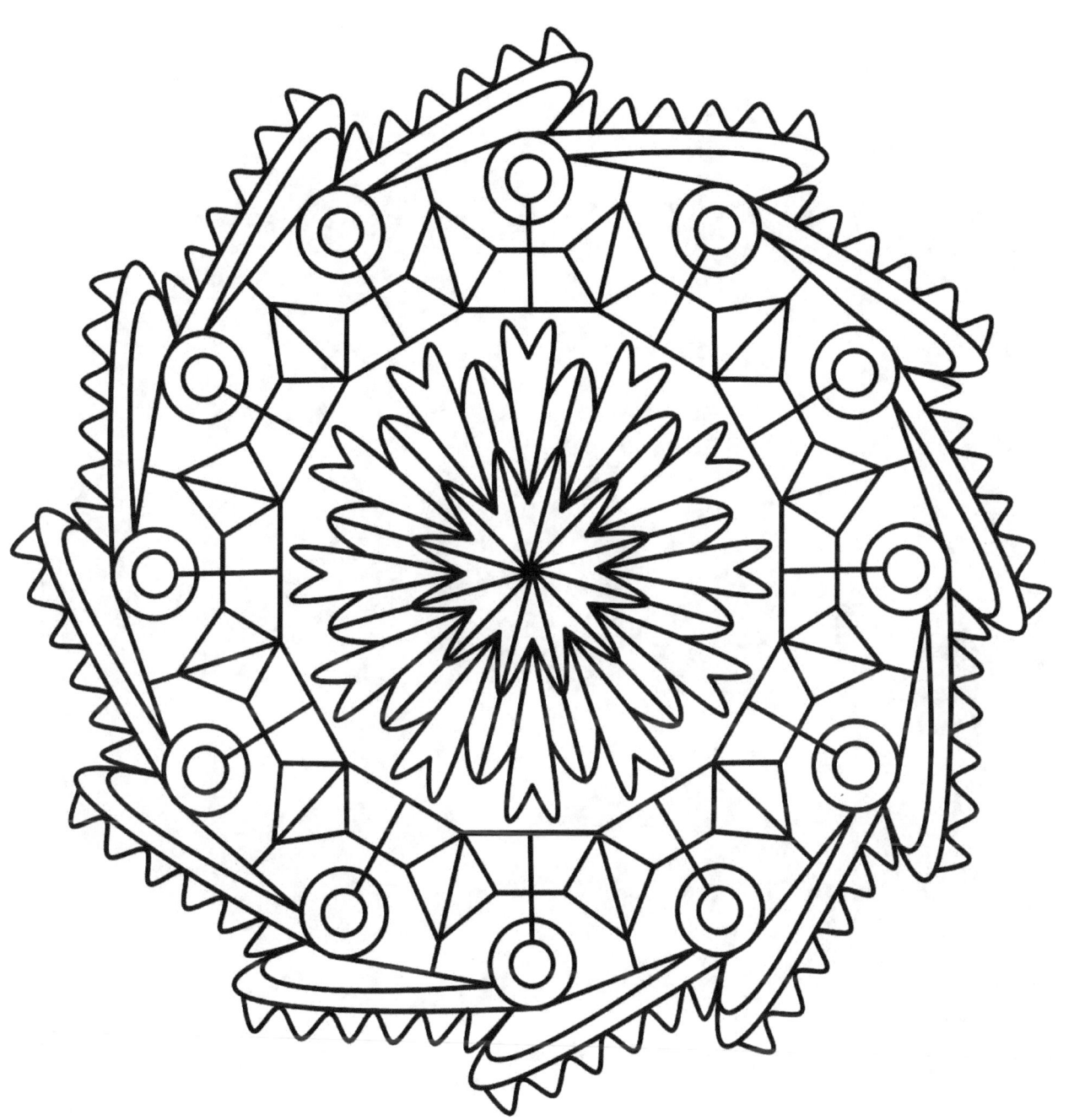

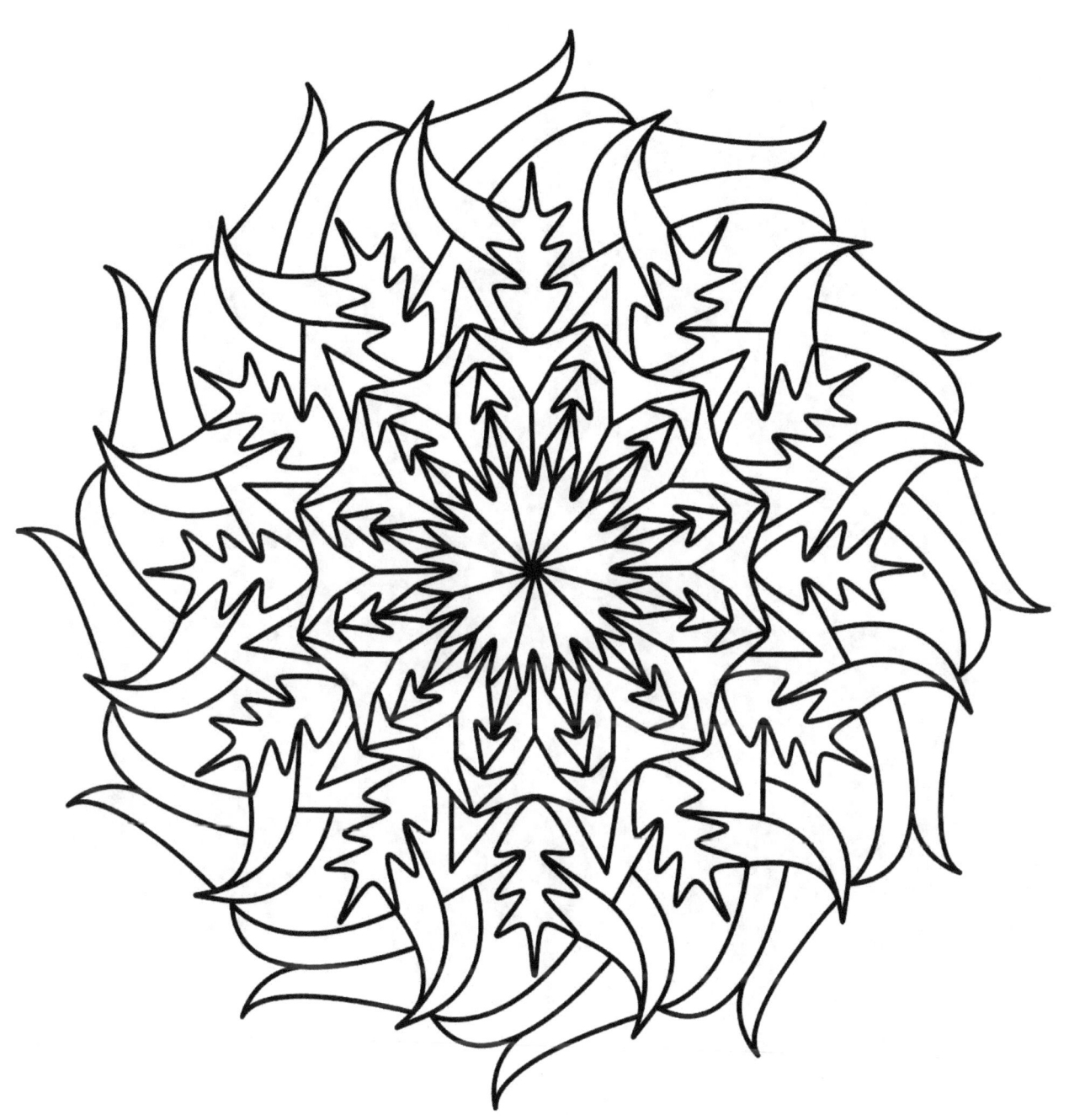

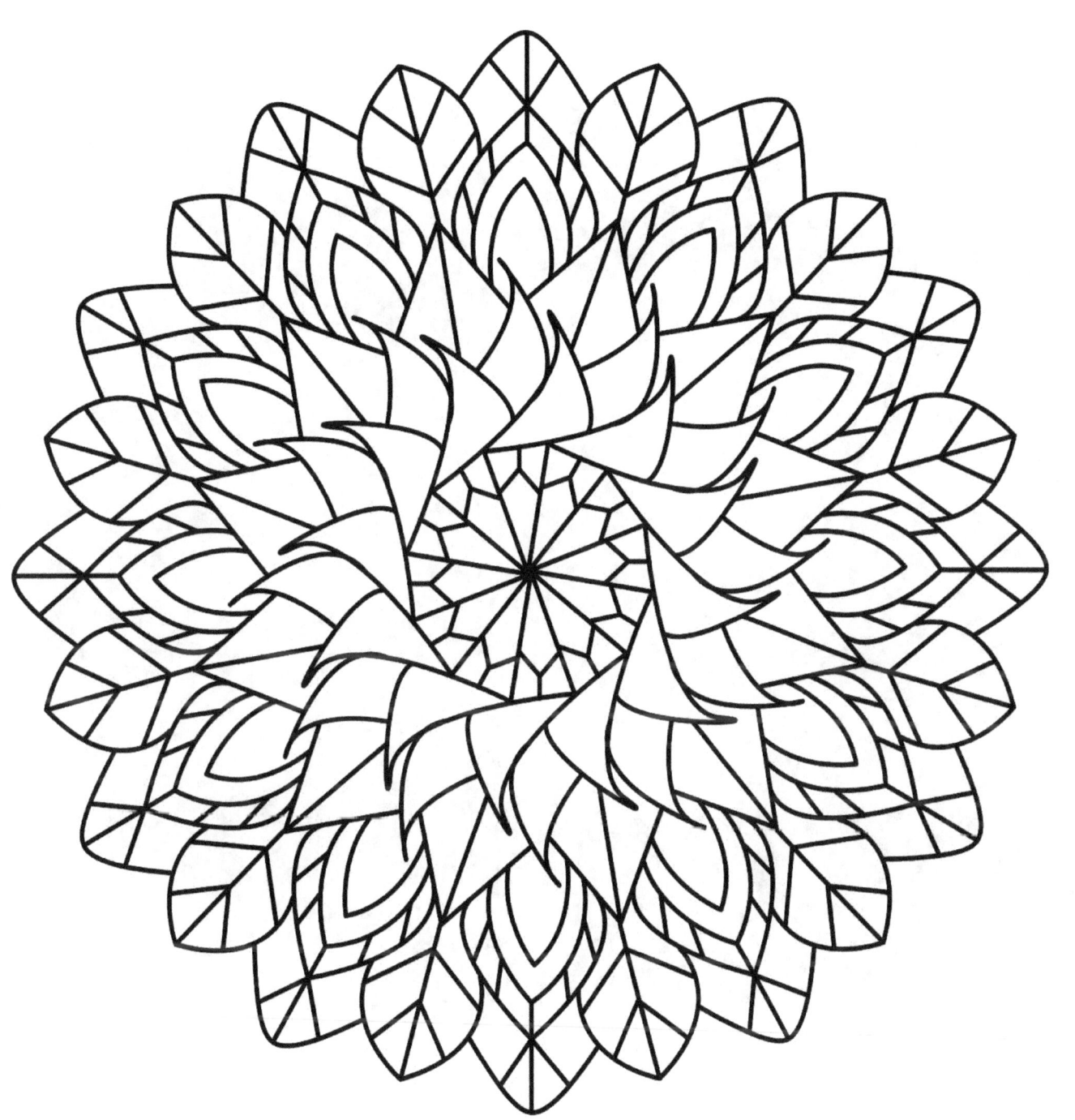

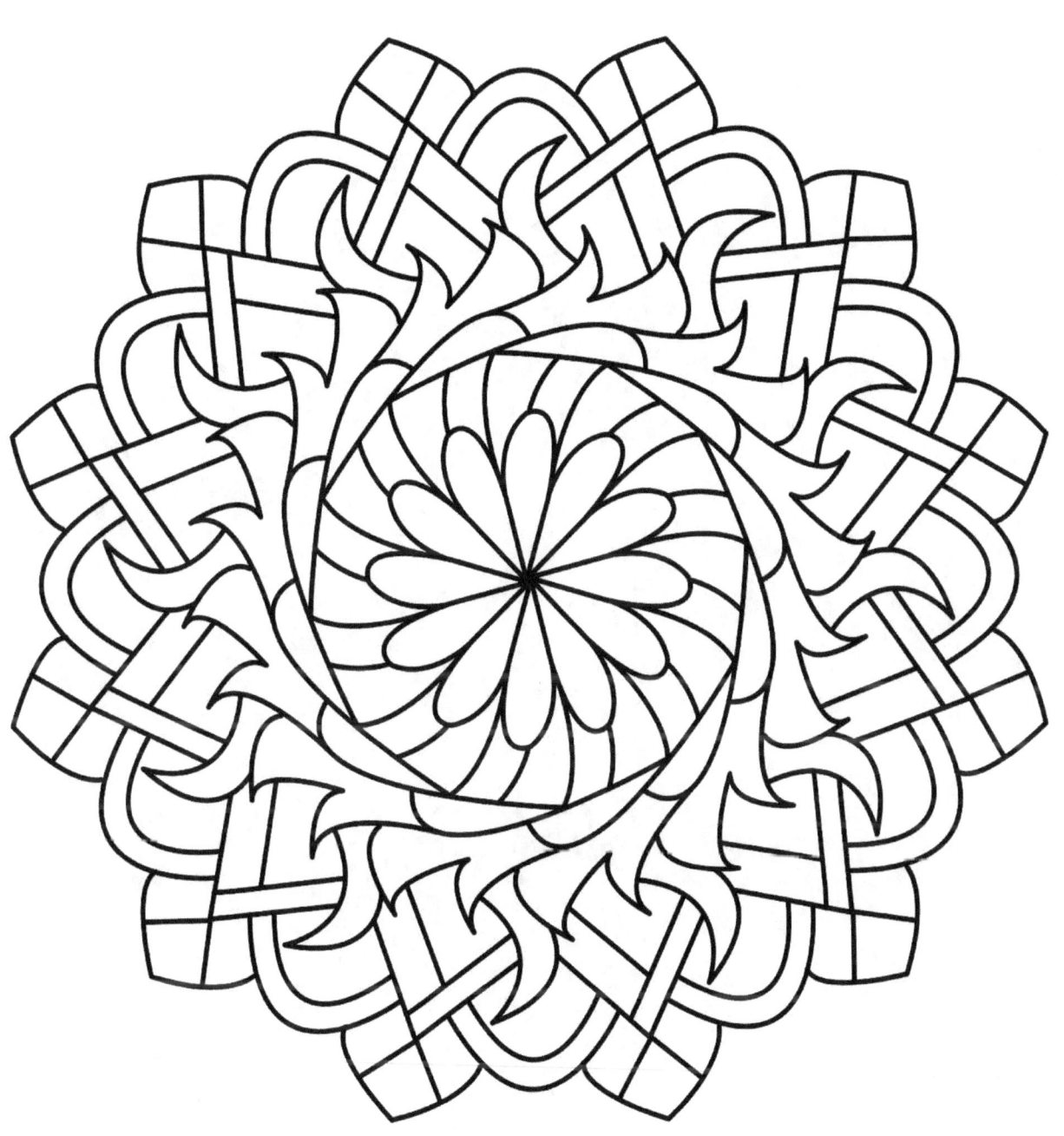

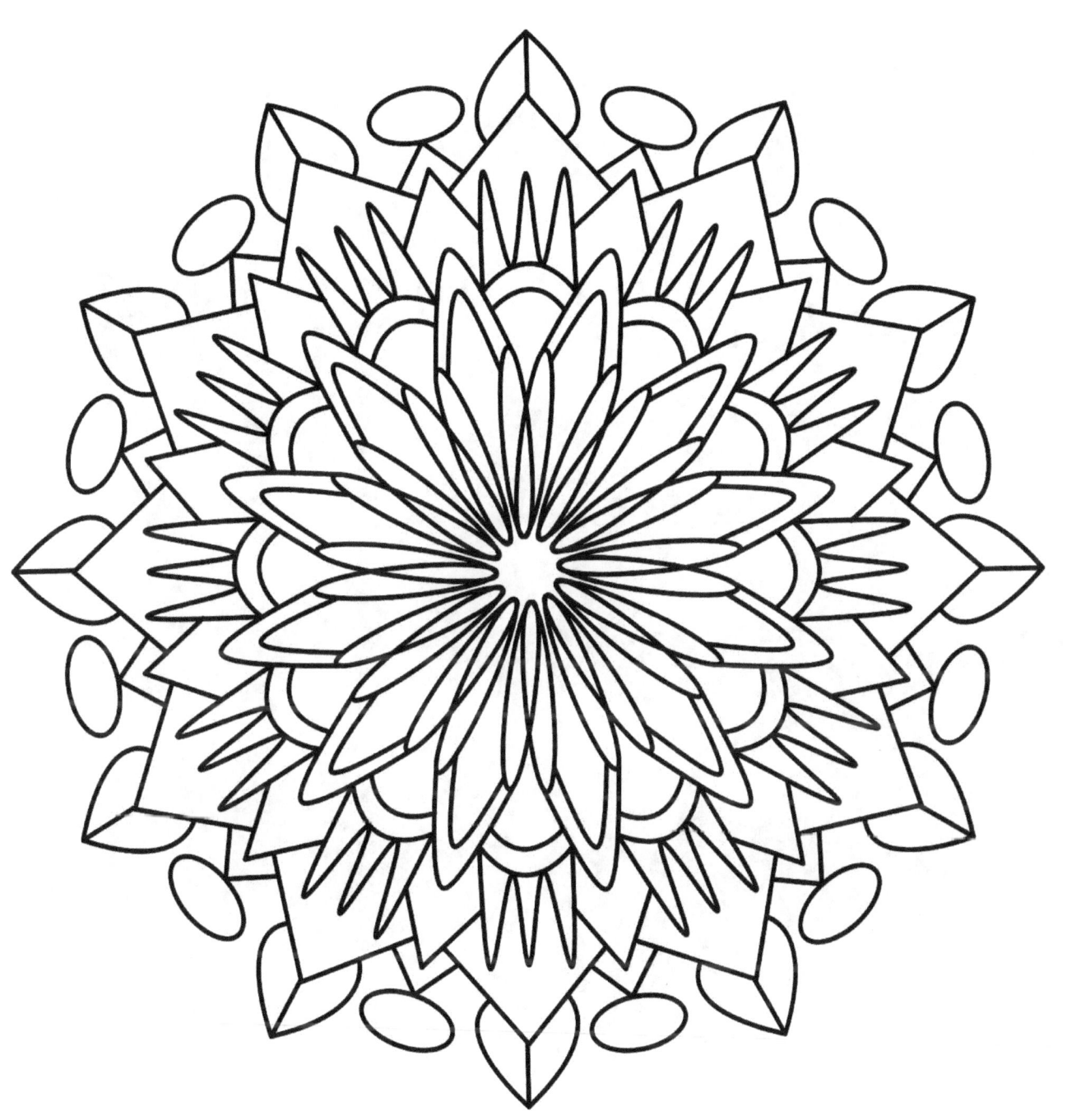

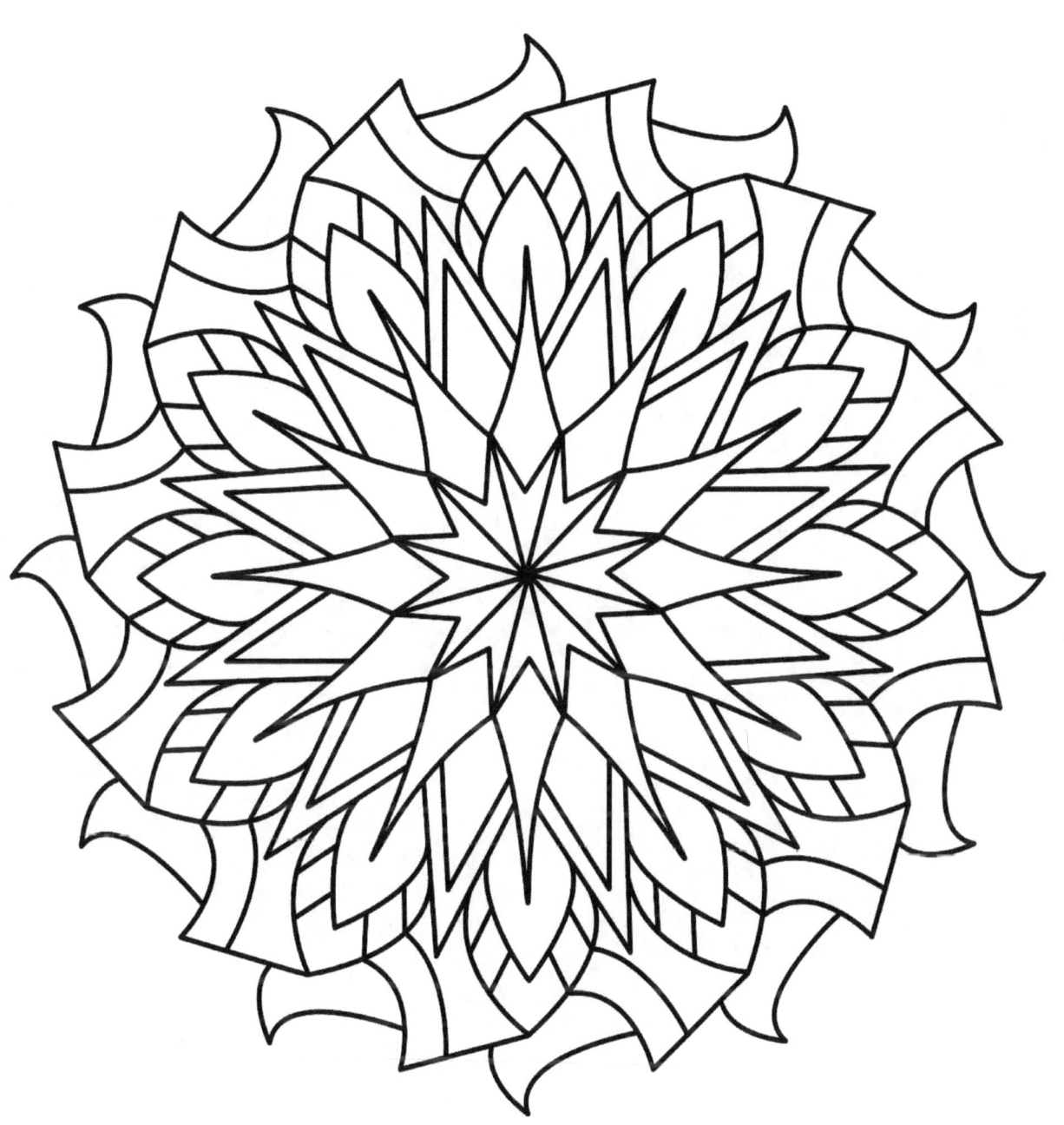

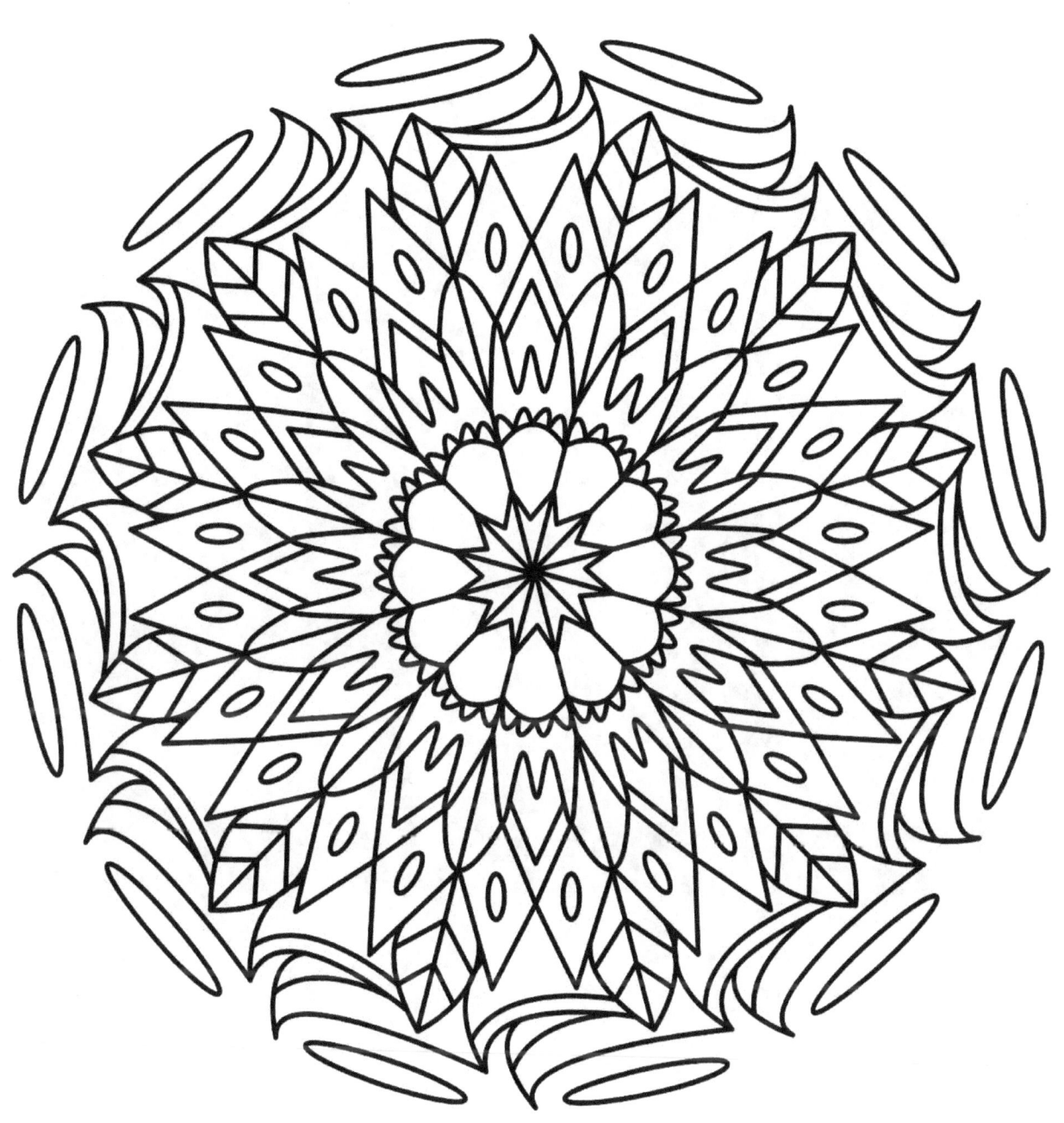

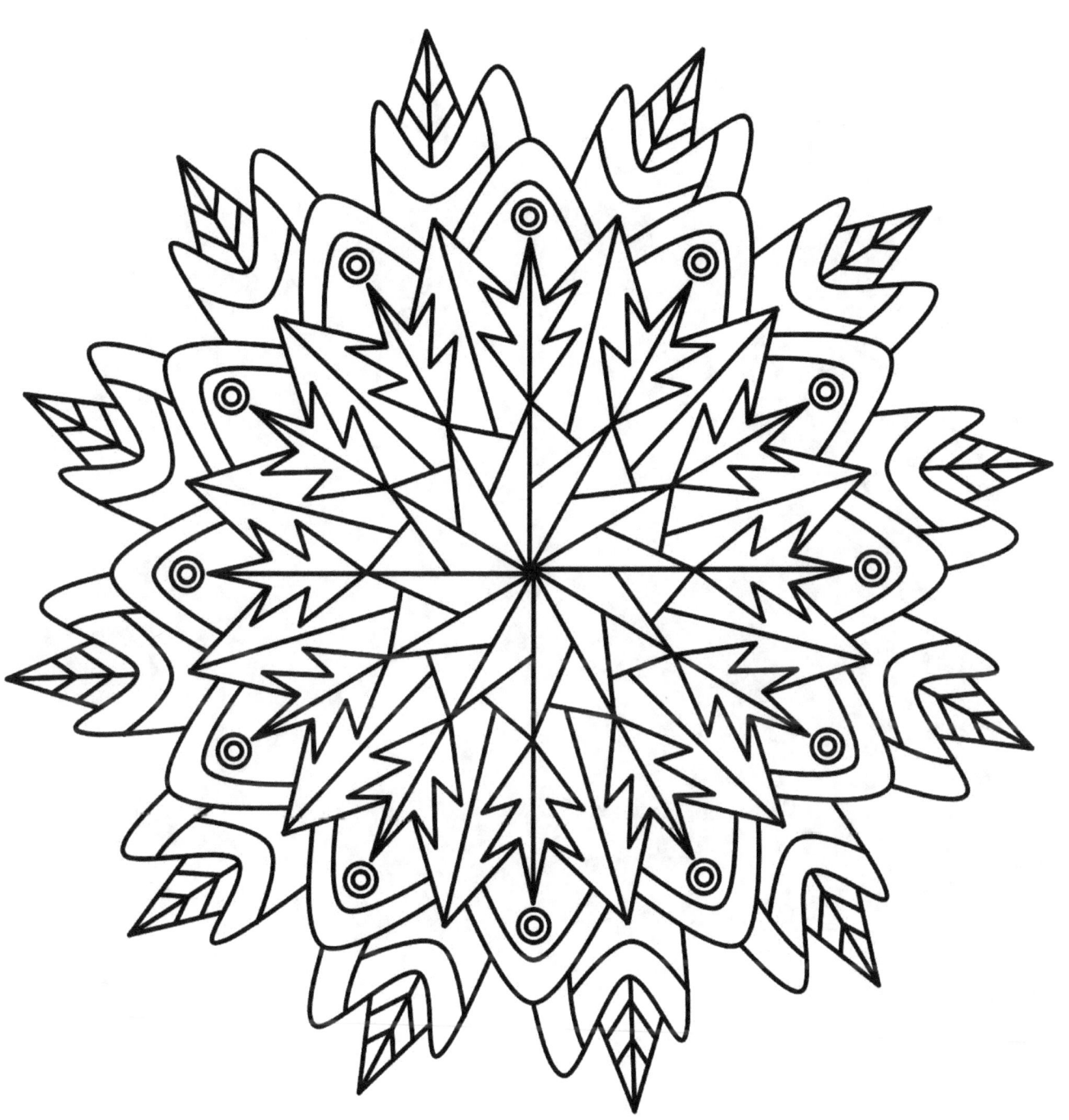

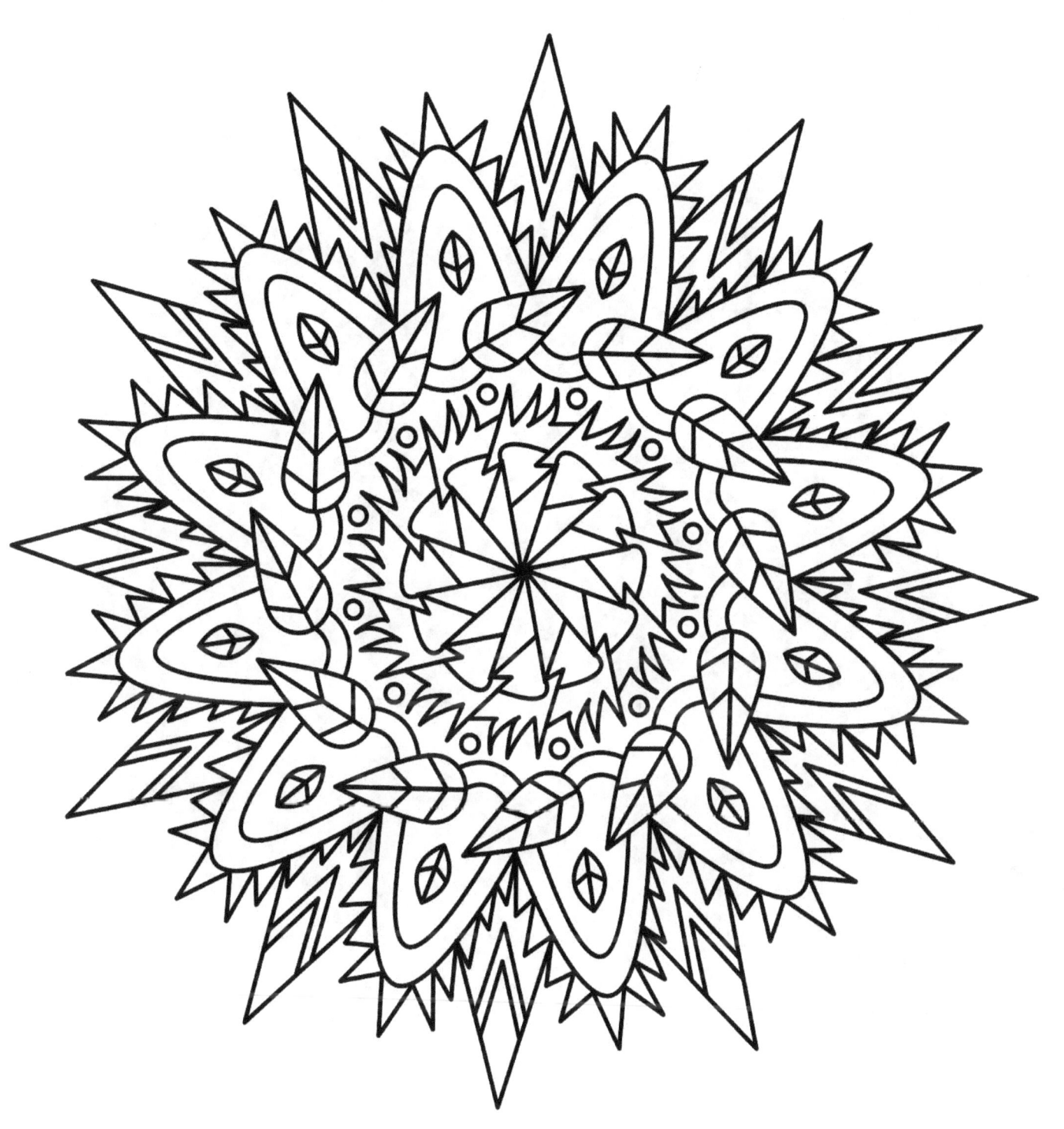

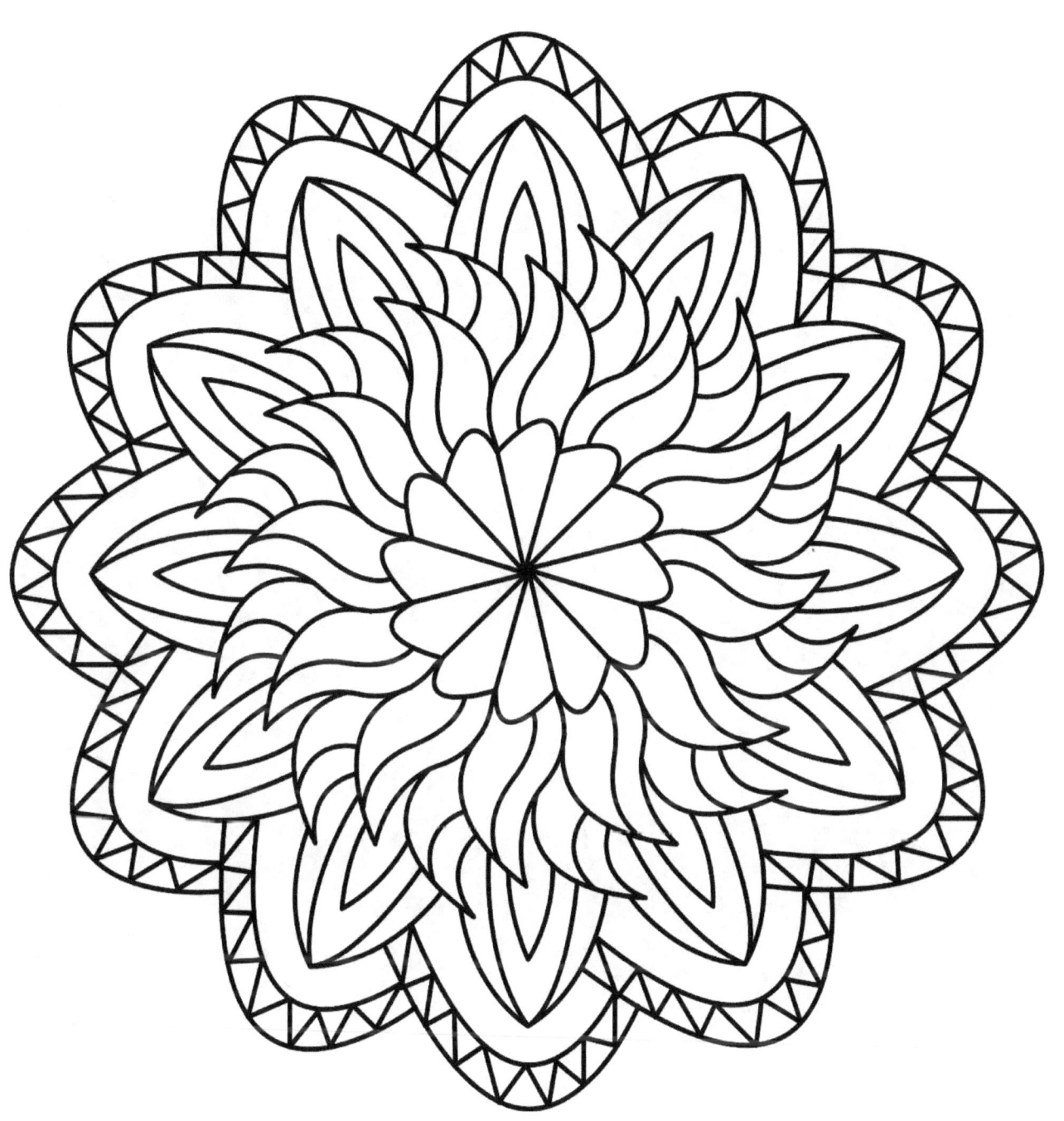

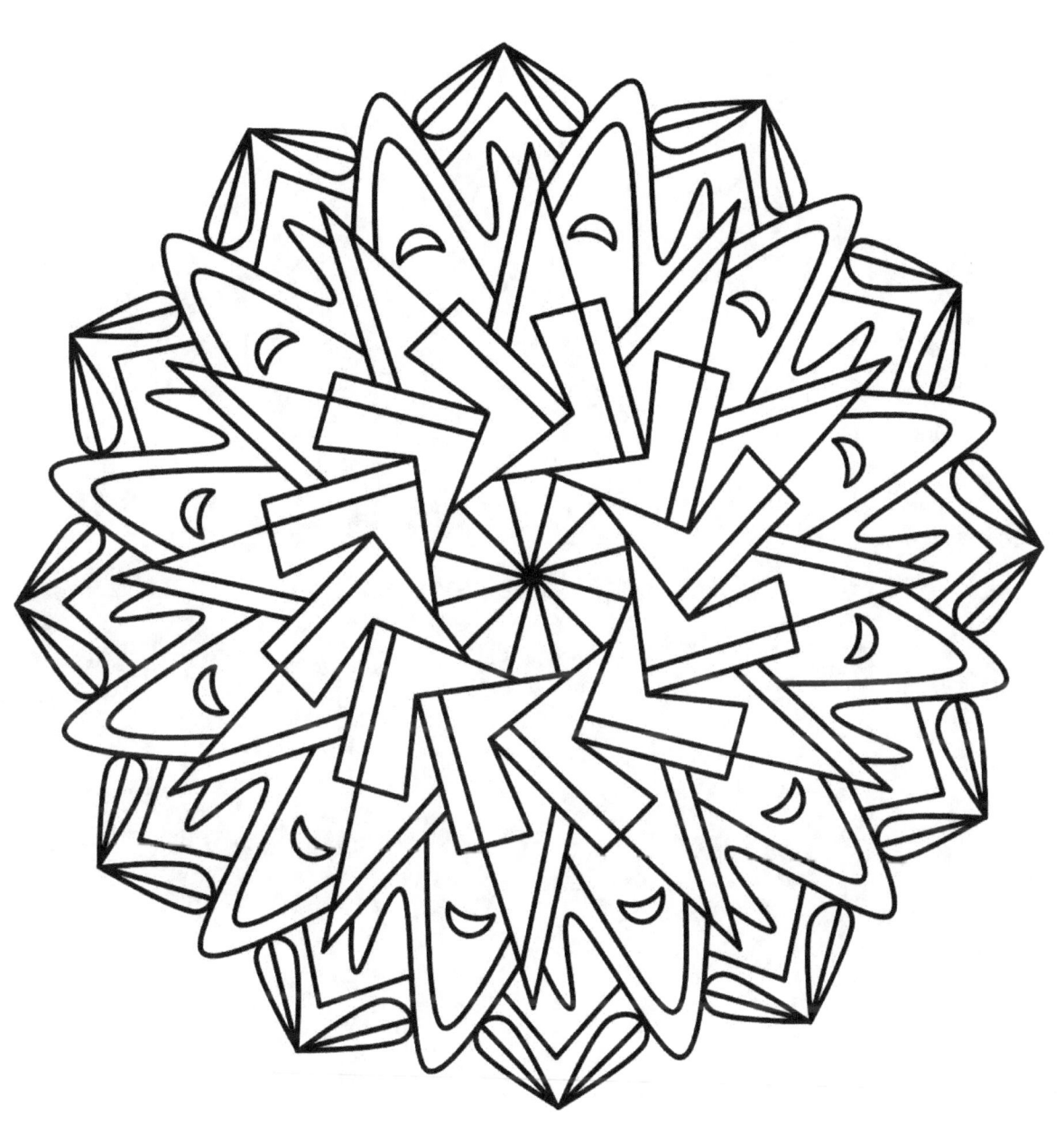

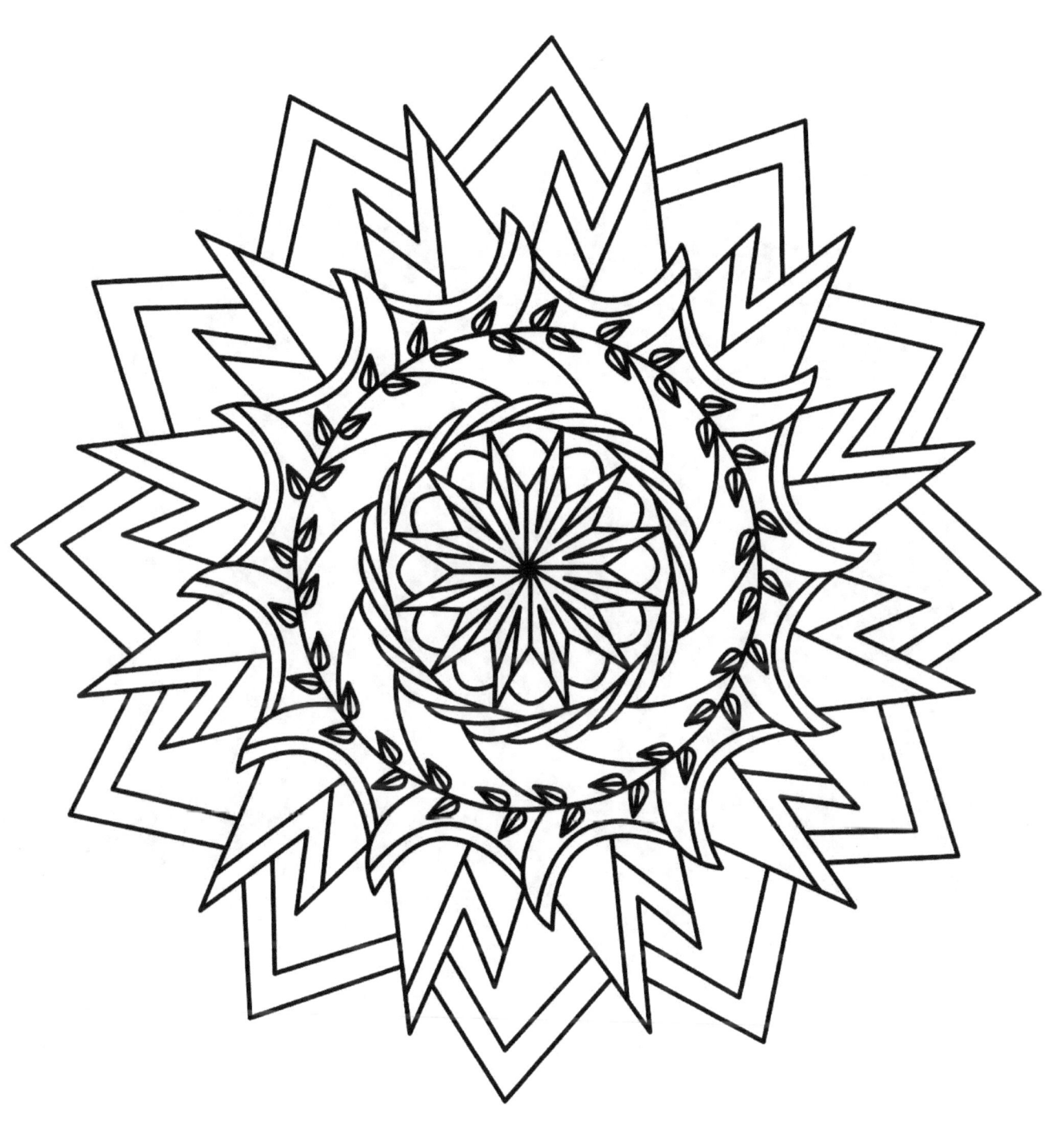

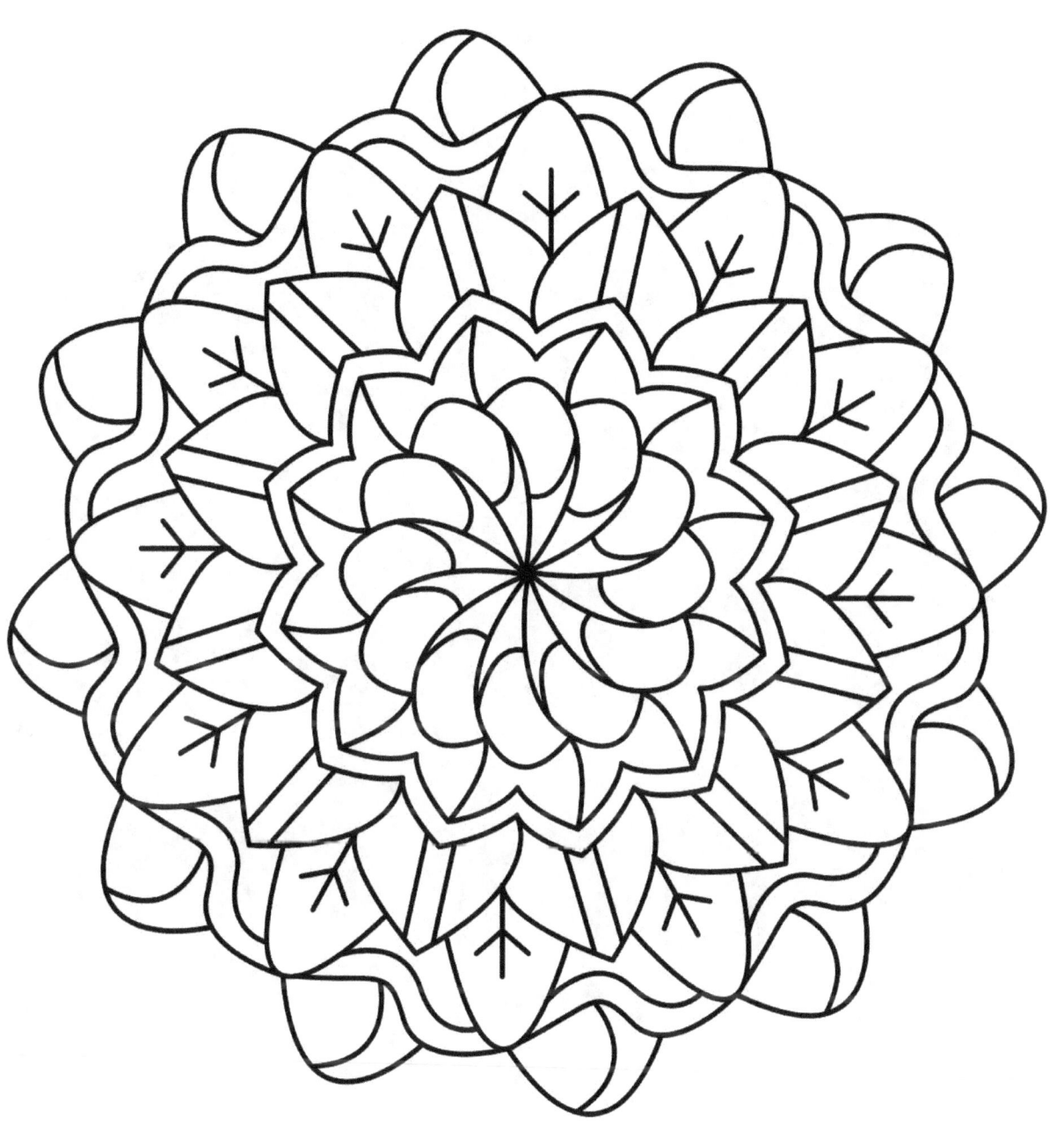

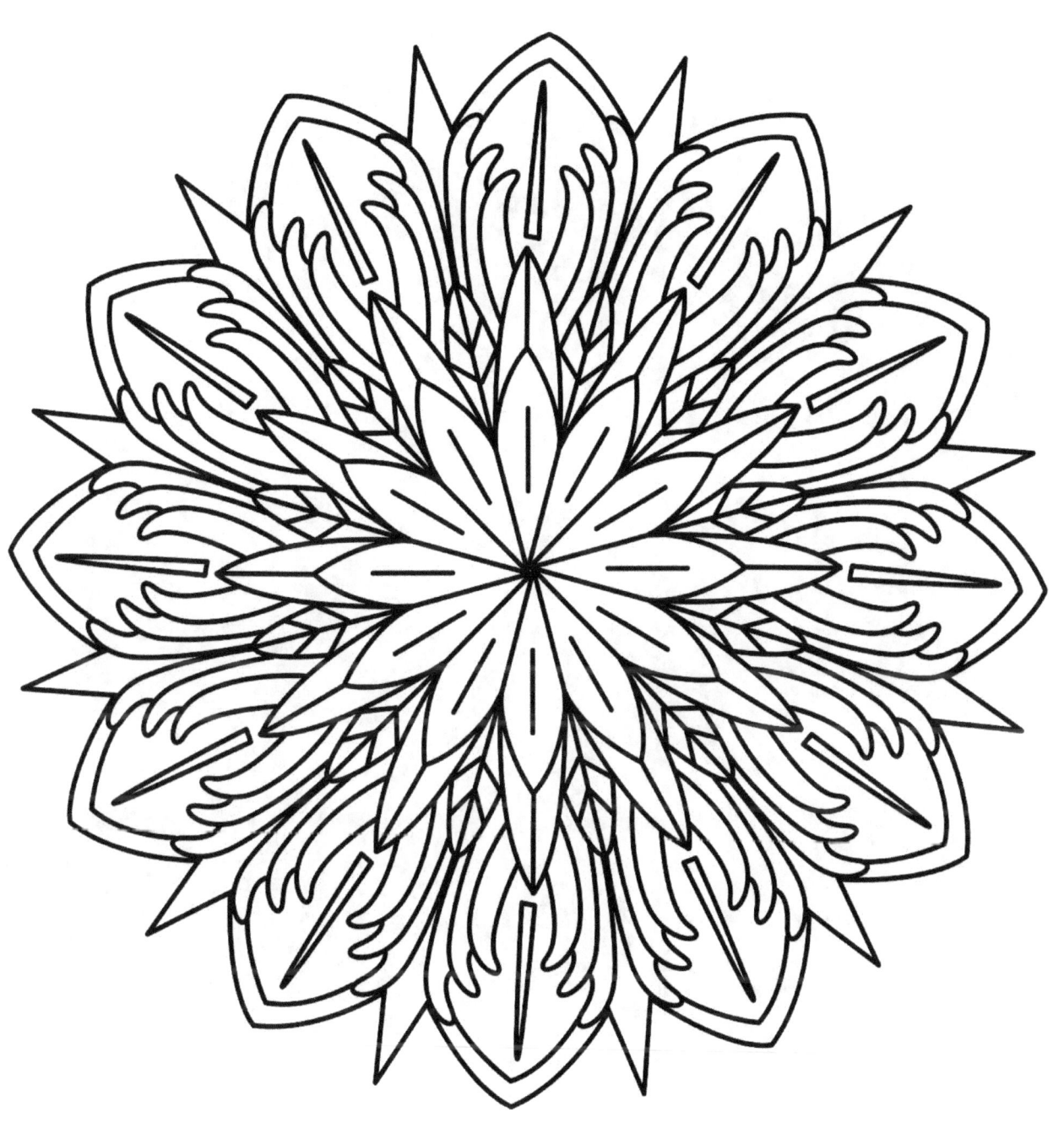

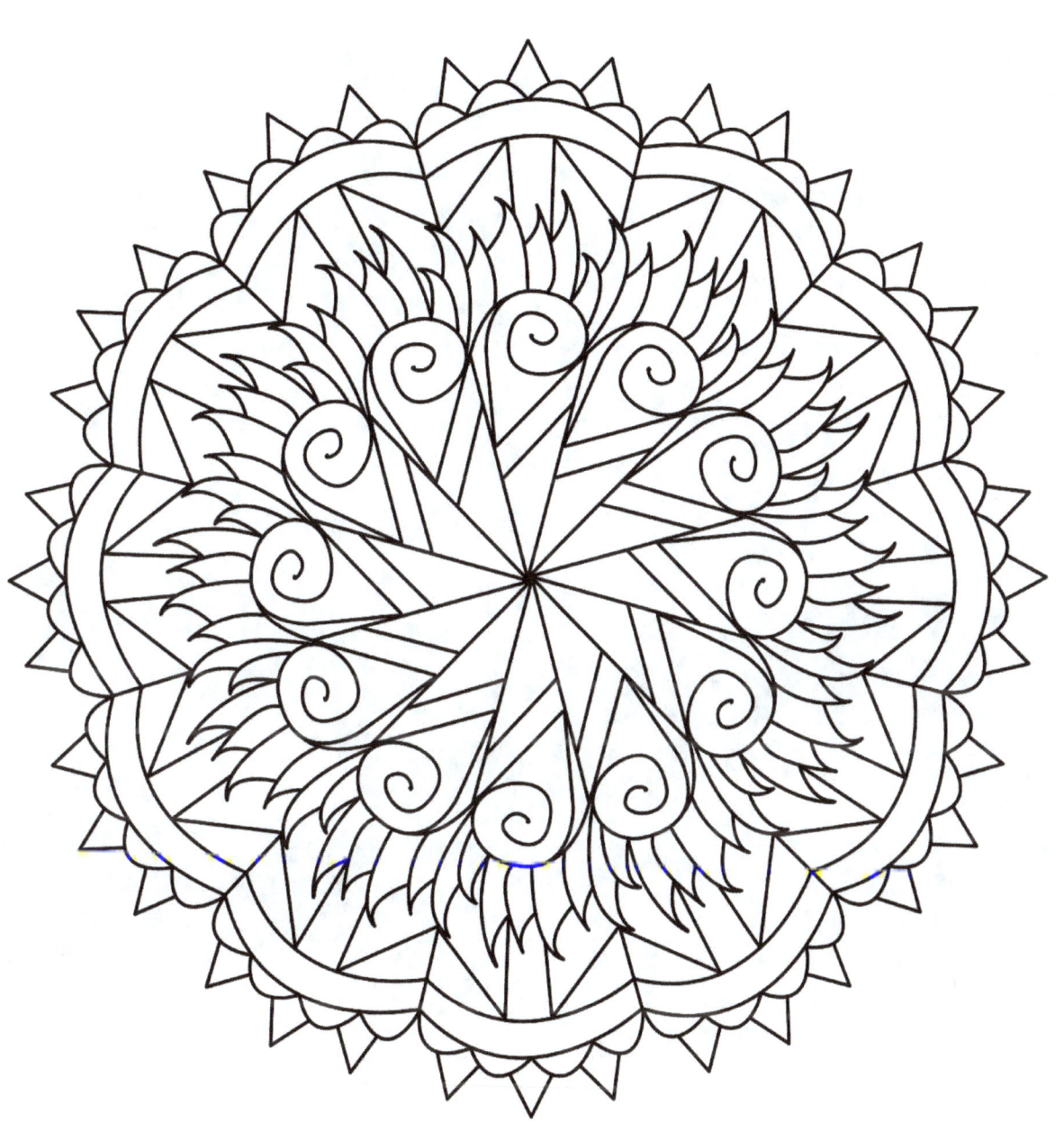

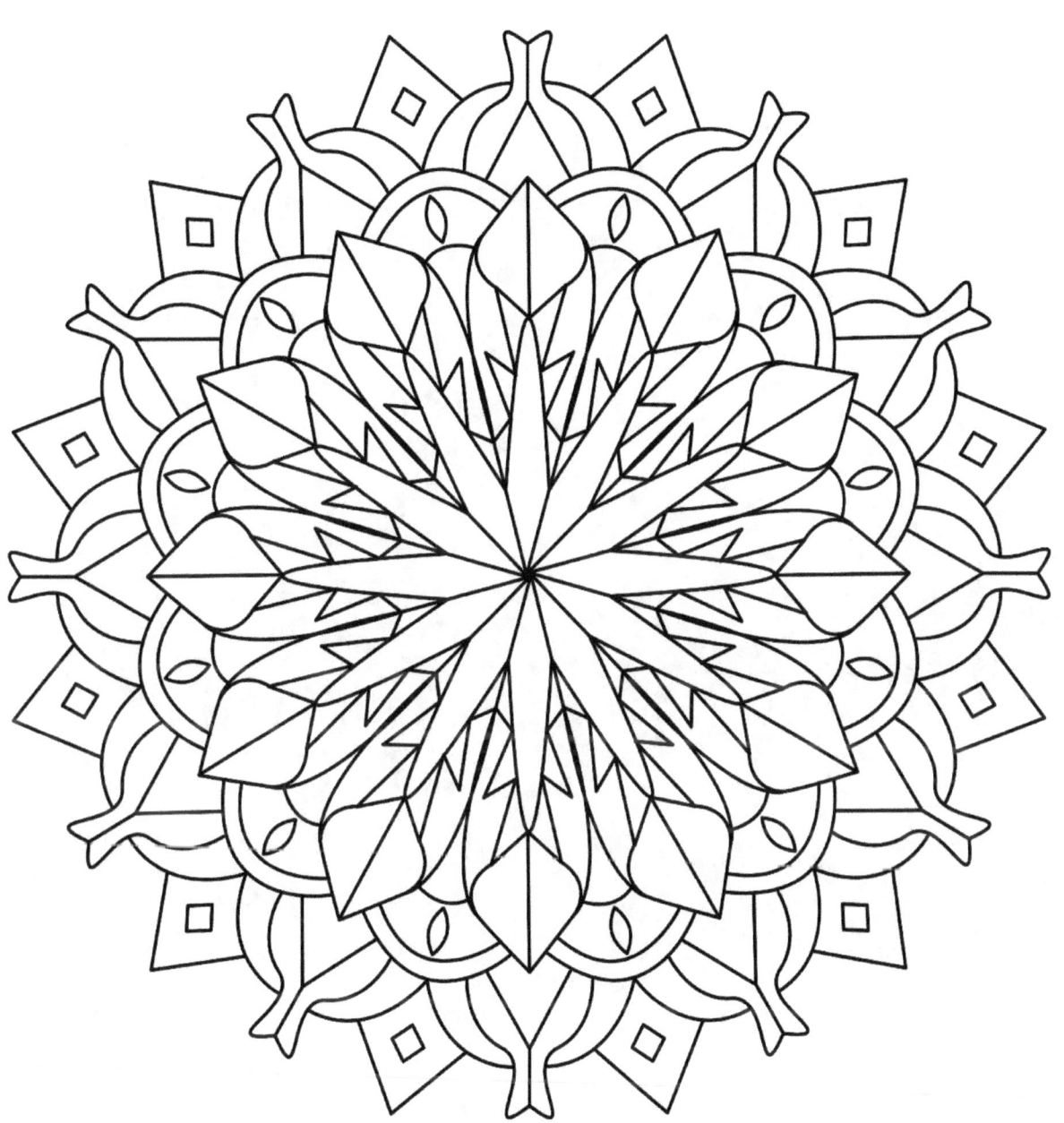

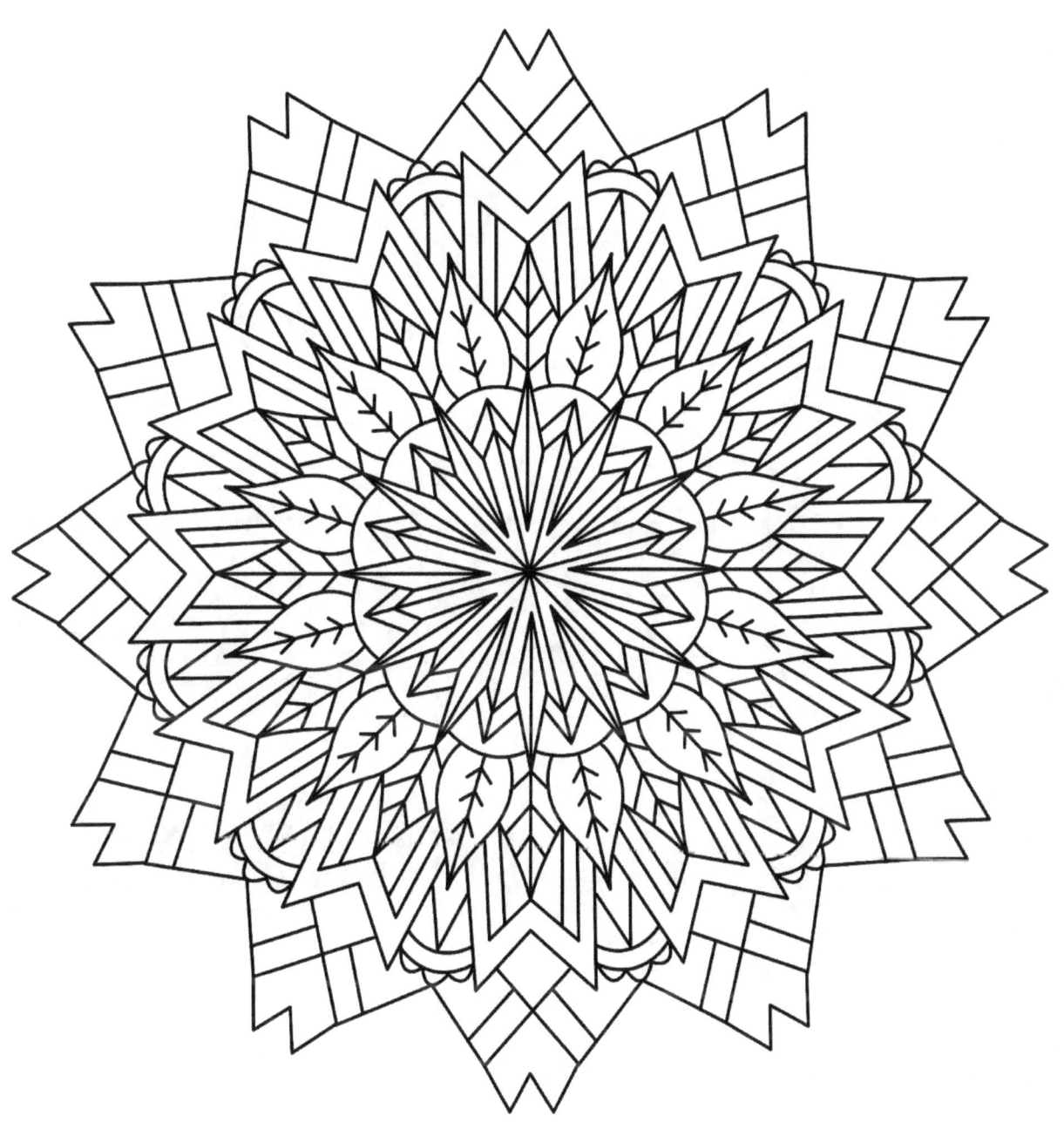

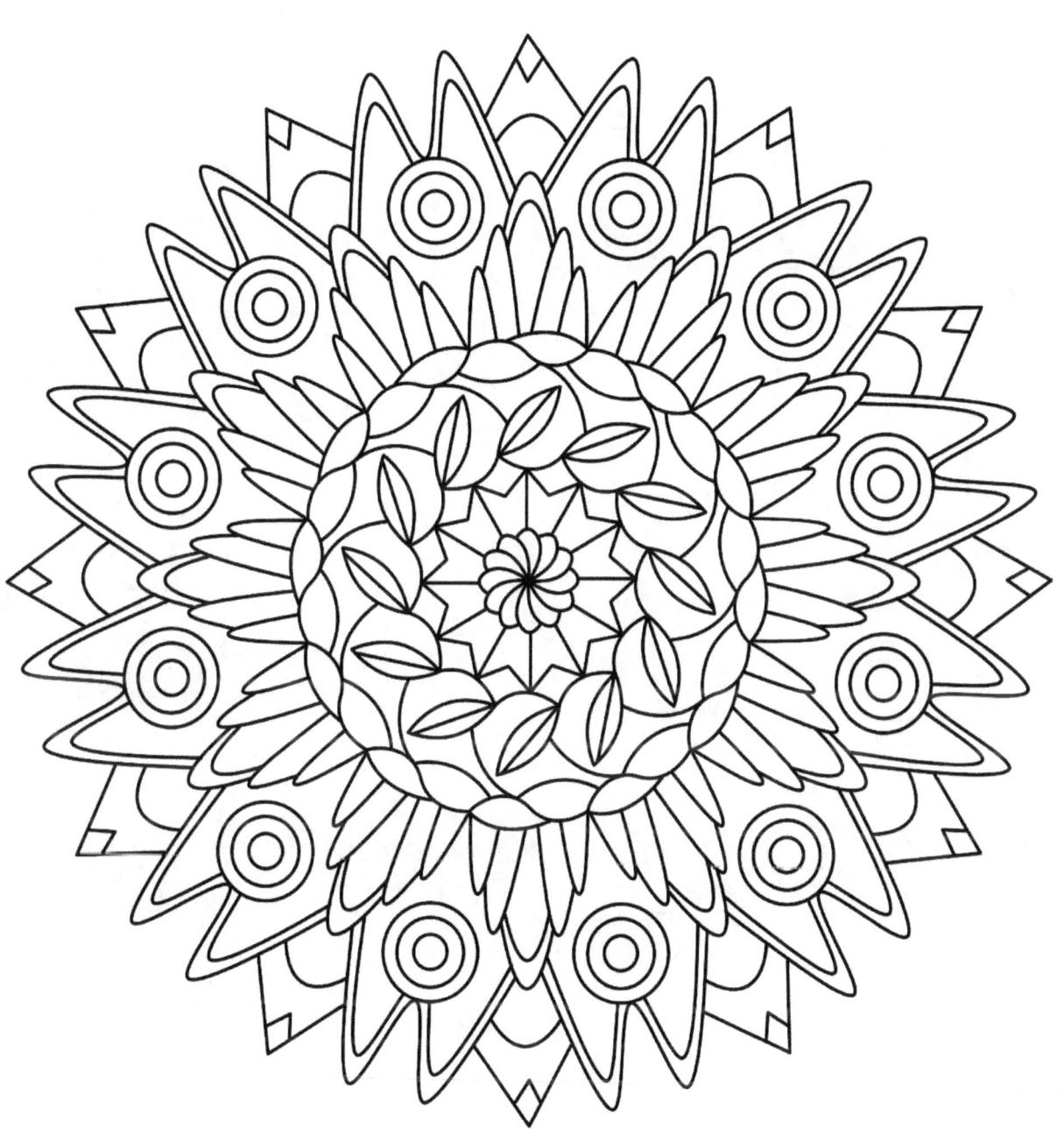

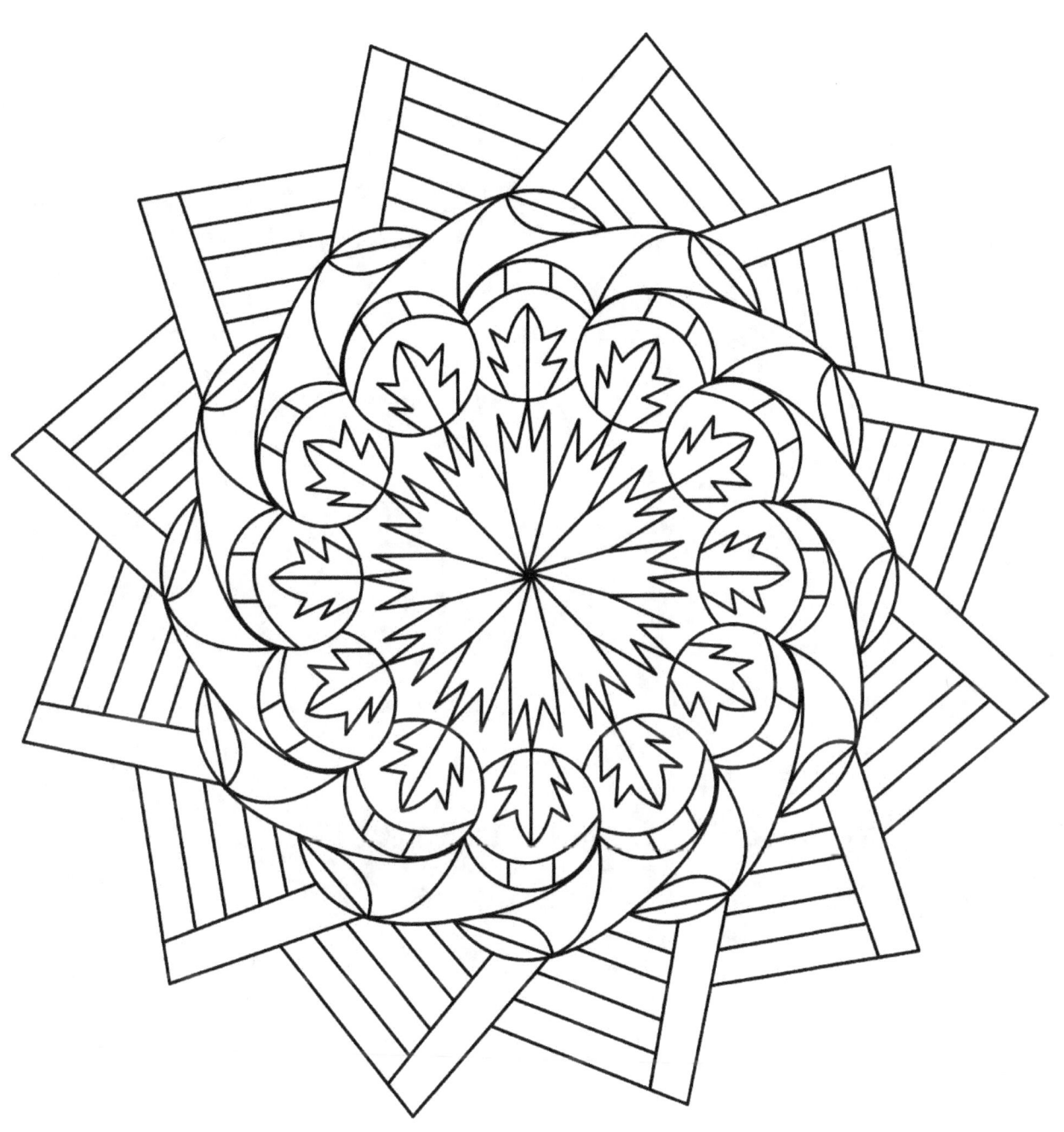

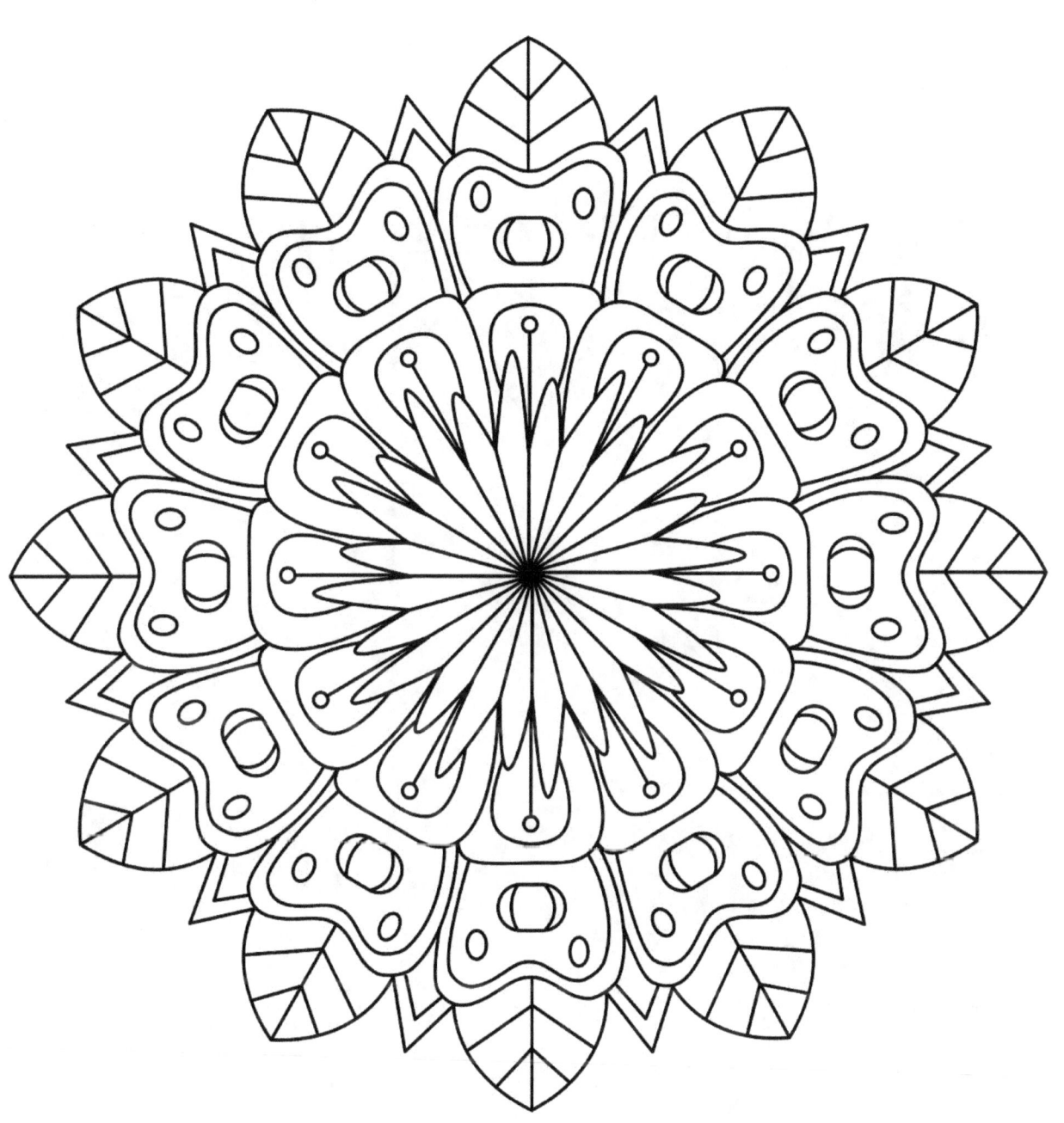

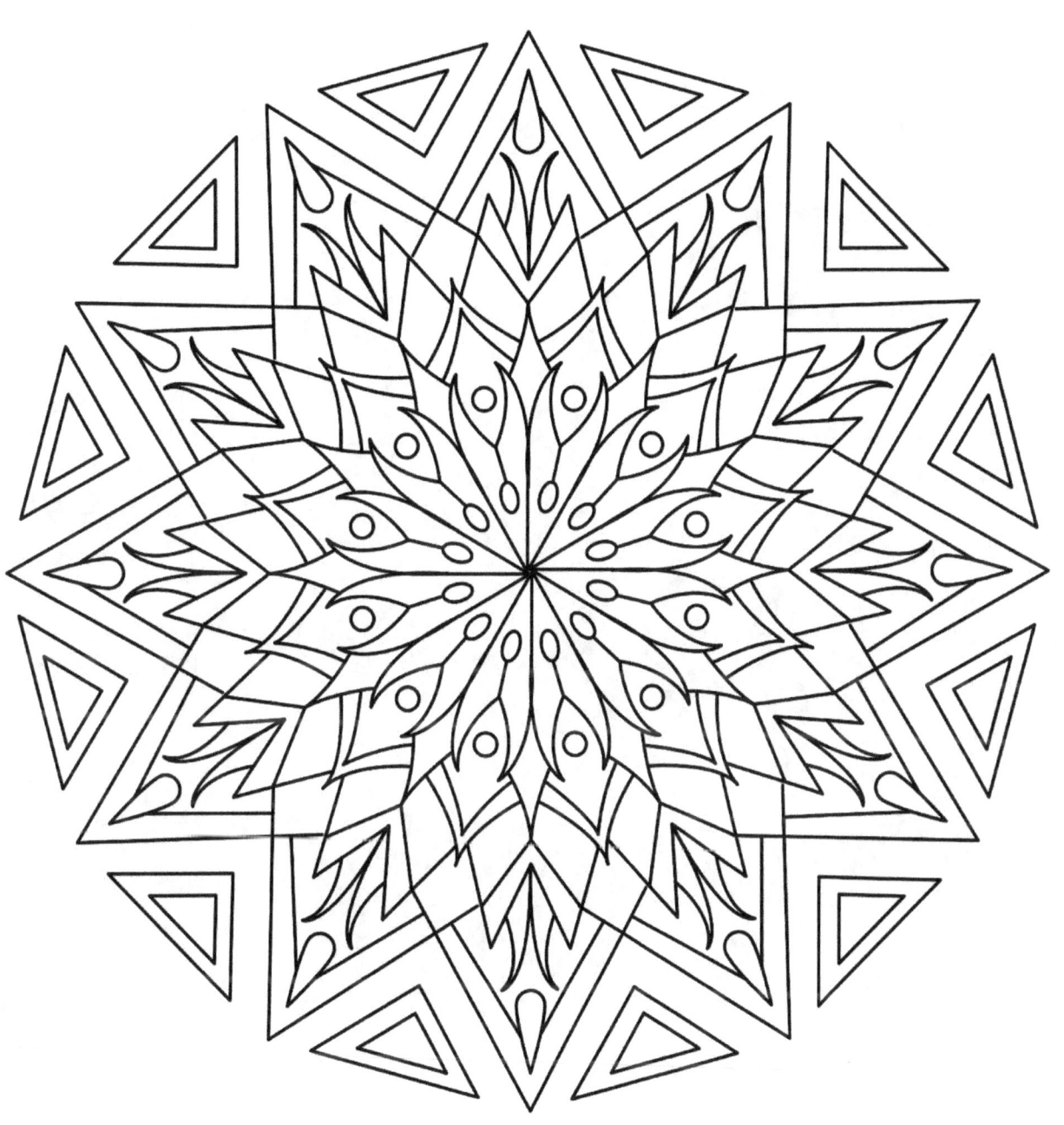

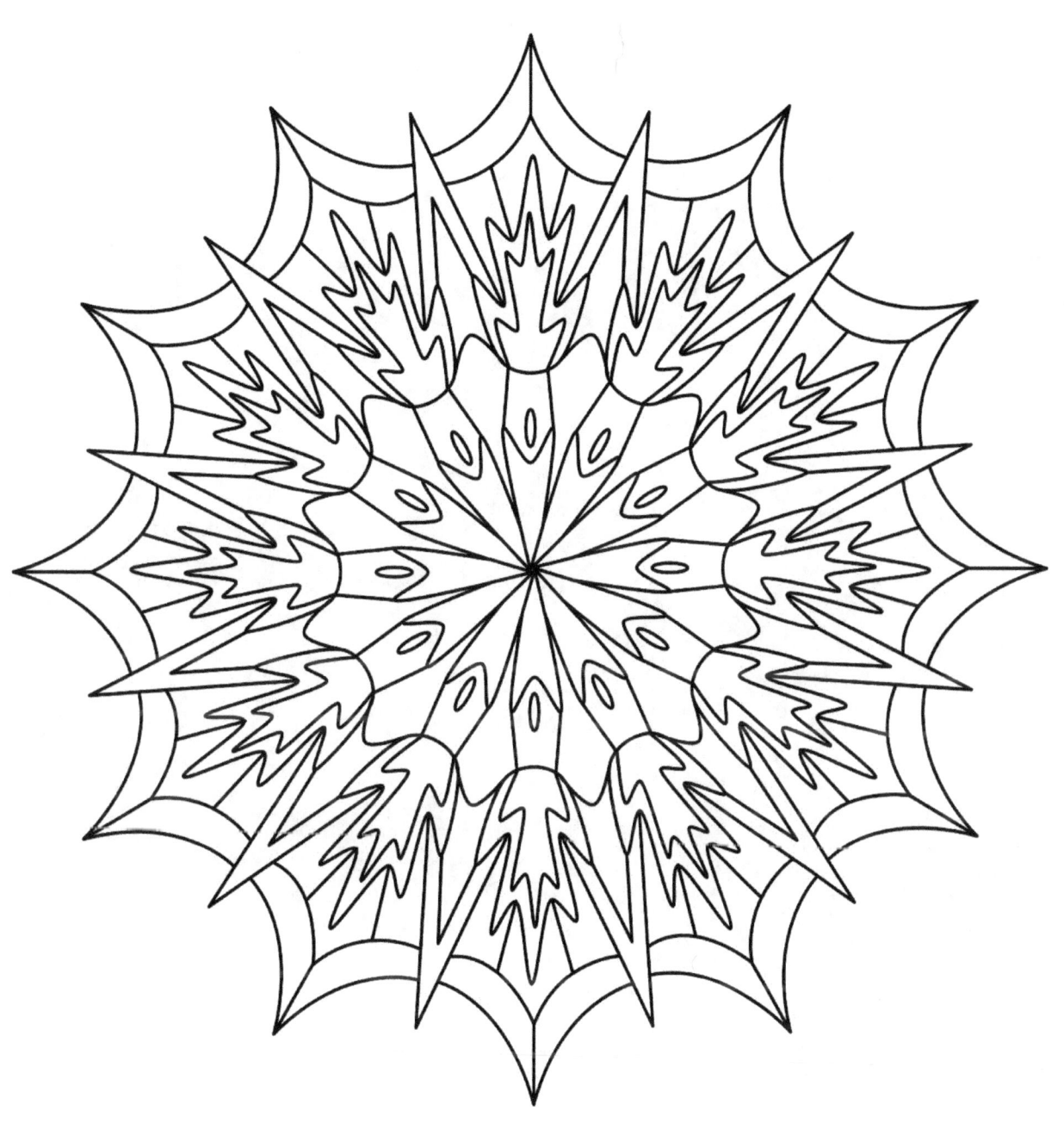

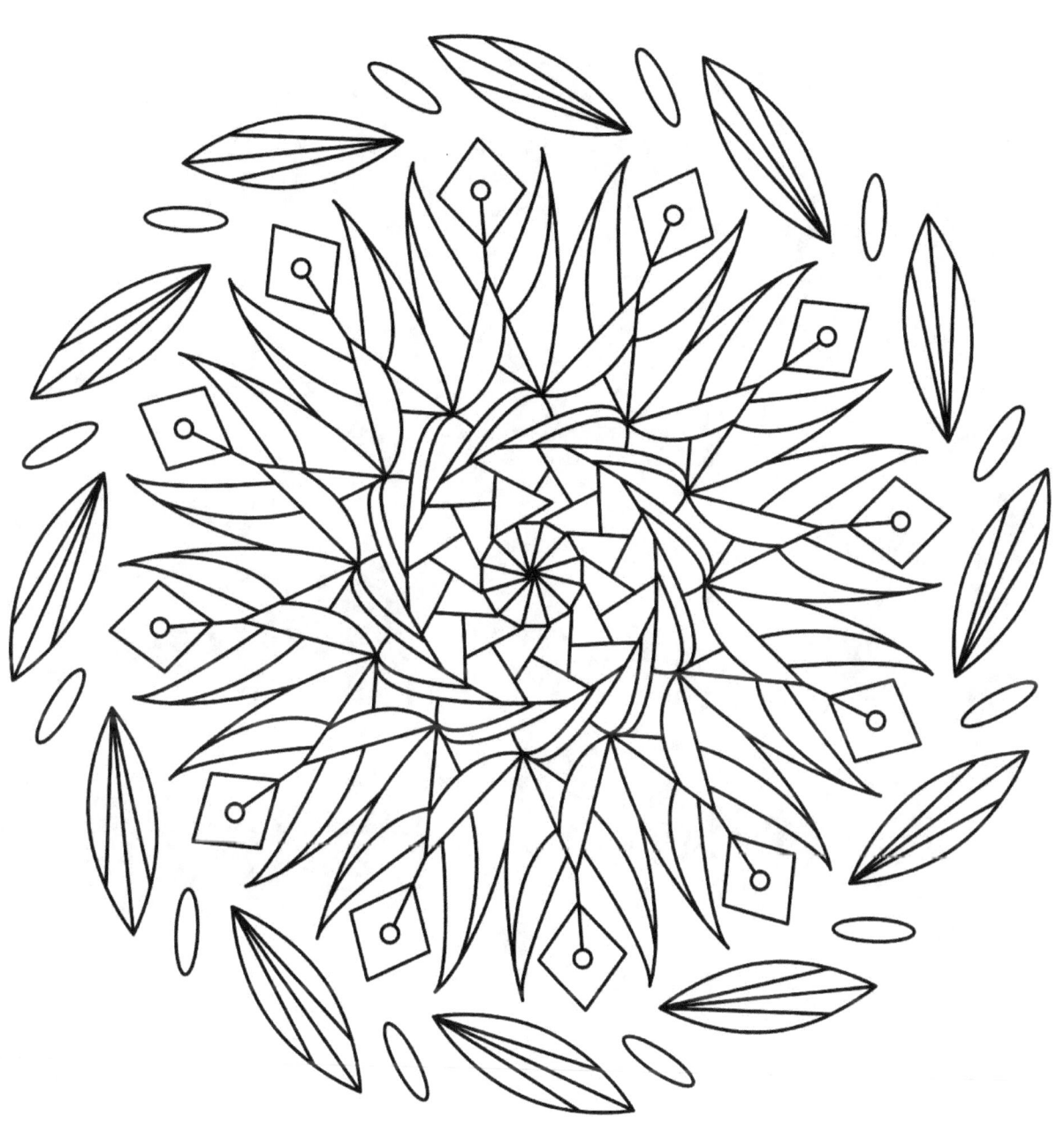

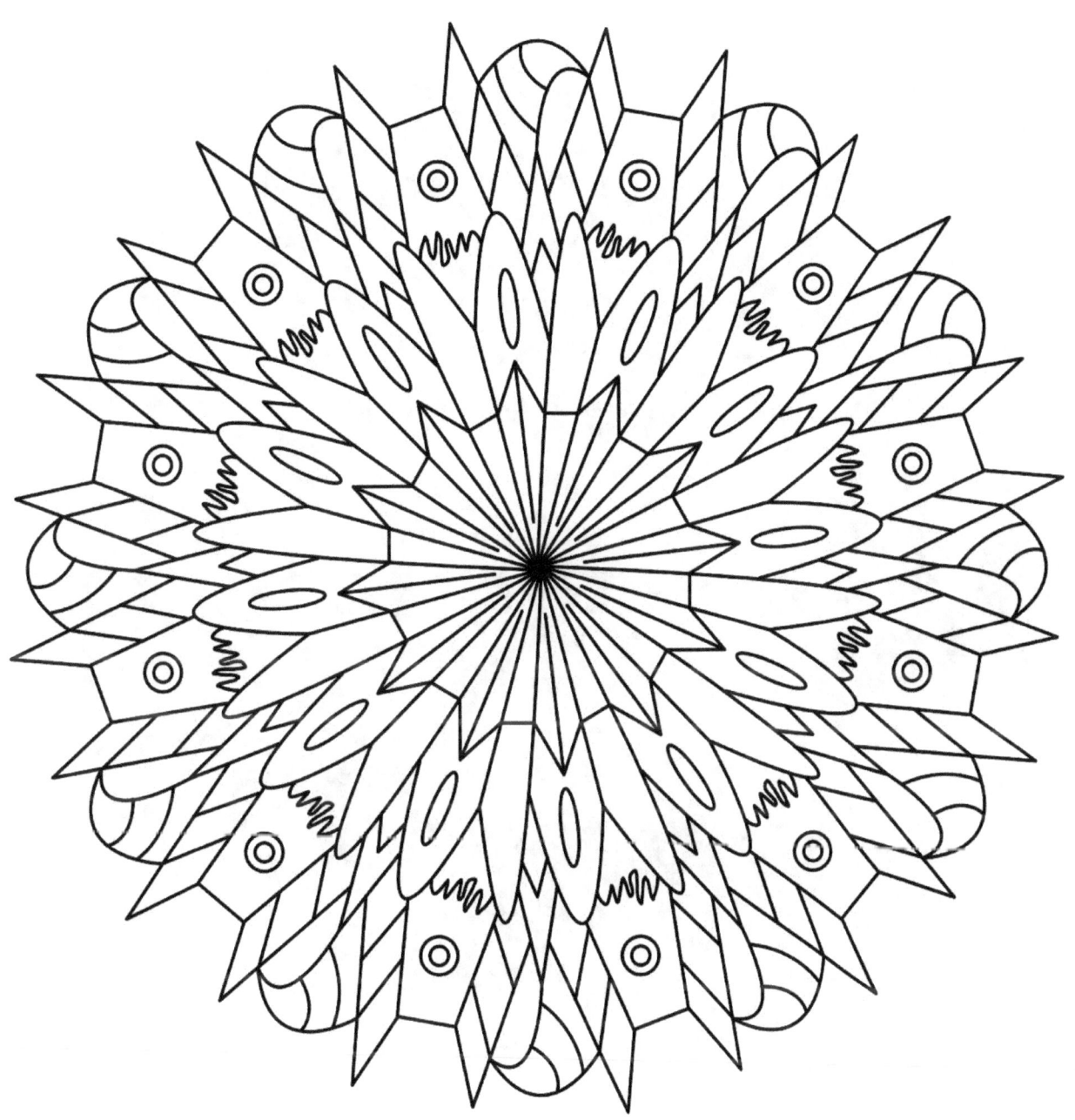

www.ingramcontent.com/pod-product-compliance
Lightning Source LLC
Chambersburg PA
CBHW081009170526

45158CB00010B/2974